GARDENING
—— for the Small Property ——

JACK KRAMER

Fulcrum Publishing
Golden, Colorado

Library of Congress Cataloging-in-Publication Data

Kramer, Jack, 1927–
        Gardening for the small property / Jack Kramer.
                p.   cm.
        Includes bibliographical references (p.   ) and index.
        ISBN 1-55591-084-X
        1. Landscape gardening.   2. Gardening.   I. Title.
    SB473.K732   1994
    635.9'67—dc20   93–43100
                                                              CIP

Printed in the United States of America

0   9   8   7   6   5   4   3   2   1

Fulcrum Publishing
350 Indiana Street, Suite 350
Golden, Colorado 80401-5093
800/992-2908

CONTENTS

TABLE OF PLANT LISTS

ACKNOWLEDGMENTS

I wish to offer thanks to the many companies that have furnished helpful information and photos of their products for this book.

CALIFORNIA REDWOOD ASSOCIATION

CALIFORNIA ASSOCIATION OF NURSERYMEN

WESTINGHOUSE ELECTRIC COMPANY

SCOTT SEED COMPANY

SEYMOUR SMITH & SONS TOOL COMPANY

LEE L. WOODARD SONS, INC.

USDA Plant Hardiness Zone Map

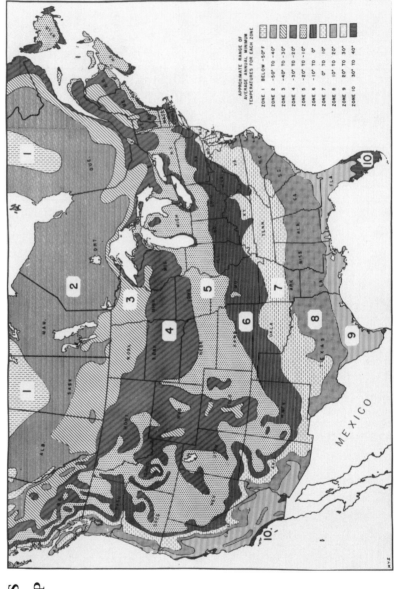

APPROXIMATE RANGE OF
AVERAGE ANNUAL MINIMUM
TEMPERATURES FOR EACH ZONE

ZONE 1   BELOW −50°F
ZONE 2   −50° TO −40°
ZONE 3   −40° TO −30°
ZONE 4   −30° TO −20°
ZONE 5   −20° TO −10°
ZONE 6   −10° TO 0°
ZONE 7   0° TO 10°
ZONE 8   10° TO 20°
ZONE 9   20° TO 30°
ZONE 10 30° TO 40°

MEXICO

INTRODUCTION

*T*oday the average property is smaller than even a few years ago. Yet it is more important to our daily living than in former times. Even on a limited site most people want a garden, a retreat from a busy, crowded world. With land space dwindling around us daily, your own special garden, small though it may be, is almost a necessity.

Landscaping as we knew it in the past—vast grounds with elaborate gardens—hardly exists now. Today's small property calls for clever arrangement and design. It calls for low maintenance, yet beauty; low cost, yet functional space. New concepts of gardening are necessary to transform the small site into a functional *and* beautiful setting to serve you and your family.

For the small garden it is essential to use appropriate trees and shrubs—plants that are in scale with the site. Pavings make the area seem larger and at the same time are inexpensive and easy to maintain. It is important to pick the best plants, for limited space does not allow too many errors.

This book is about planning the small garden to provide a place for relaxing, for dining or for viewing as a pretty picture from the house. Designing the small property means framing your house with trees, shrubs and flowers in a happy marriage of form, texture and color.

If all these benefits sound like a big order from a small garden, read on. It can be done. In this book we hope to show and tell you how to do it reasonably and with low maintenance for maximum pleasure.

Chapter One

YOUR PROPERTY AND YOU

*L*andscaping is basically shaping the property to your uses—additional space for dining, relaxing, playing or for growing plants. (At the same time it must create an aesthetically inviting setting.) The basic premise of planning the property is putting it to work for you. What you want and how you shape it depends on the site, budget, weather and climate.

If you can afford one, call in a landscape architect for a few consultations to get you started. (This is not terribly expensive for a small property.) Then you can follow the plan and add your own alterations over many years. A good garden design is a result of time and thoroughness rather than haste and expediency.

A new property needs certain basics, such as drainage and grading, that will require attention before you do any planning. It is wise to start right—do the things that should be done and must be done—to avoid trouble later. You have probably heard this admonition a hundred times, but it is worth repeating.

For an old house, only minor attention to drainage and grading is generally necessary, for land curves and excess water drainage have already been well established.

FIRST LOOK AT THE PROPERTY

Before you decide on any garden plan, walk your property several times. Use the contractor's plot to determine where the boundaries are, which way the site faces and whether it is level or flat. Consider the view you have—if any—and seek out natural level changes that can be exploited to your benefit. Observe how close the neighbors are to see if you will need fences, screens or hedges to ensure privacy. As you walk, make mental notes on whether the site is windy or calm and where there are protected areas and exposed places.

After "exploring" the property, go into the house and look at the site from a living-room window or any other rooms you occupy a good part of the time. Study the angles and vistas and seek out visually pleasing perspectives. Consider the lot as a space with small spaces within it, for a garden is several workable areas within a larger one.

If possible, visit neighbors' gardens and see what they have done. What kind of trees and shrubs have they used? Are their plantings thriving or just merely getting along? Nearby gardens, although in your same area, will not be identical. But they will be similar enough to give you an idea of what not to do. You will see things you like; remember these. Things you don't like, forget immediately.

Observe the shape of your property, for this is a clue to its arrangement. Is it long and narrow, rectangular, pie-shaped or a corner site? The shape is your starting point, because it dictates the shapes of patios and lawns and how they will relate to the overall form.

Dwarf evergreens and low plantings are used to create a fine front garden. The greenery does not overpower the house; it frames it. (Photo by Hedrich Blessing)

DRAINAGE AND GRADING

As mentioned, an old house has little or no grading and drainage problems. The garden is established, and drainage patterns and runoff systems have been there a long time, saving you much money. Alterations, such as removing and replacing trees or shrubs and modifying the site somewhat, do require work and money, but it is little in comparison to the cost or time consumed in working out a garden plan for a new home.

A new house and grounds give you freedom in your garden design, but often grading is forgotten in the excitement of the purchase. Now is the time to observe and determine what has to be done.

Many new homes have a barren setting and compacted land from heavy equipment, so the grounds are not ready for landscaping. Generally, the contractor leaves you with graded subsoil—the topsoil has been stripped and heavy machinery has compacted the soil. If the topsoil is still there (and it should be if you had a considerate contractor), it will be piled to one side someplace.

If you want a small pool or a terrace, you will need level land; a lawn requires a perfectly flat surface that has a slight pitch. Once the fence is up and shrubbery is in place, it is impossible to get equipment in to grade these areas. Determine now where you want the terrace and decide where a flat surface for a lawn is needed.

The land around your house must be graded to slope away from the building and to carry water to the nearest street, storm drain or watercourse. Be sure that the slope is in one direction, without rises or hollows. (Allow 2 inches [5 cm] to every 10 feet [3 m].) Hollows will create bogs that will accumulate water and allow nothing to grow, and rises in the land are unsightly. Rainwater must be allowed to drain off your property.

Wait until after a good rainfall to determine just how to grade or how much to grade, for then you can see exactly which way the land lies and where the water goes. If you are fortunate, there may be no problems of standing water around the house or in the front or back yards. On the other hand, there may be areas of subsoil several inches below the house that must be filled so that the slope of the land is not impeded.

To grade the property you will probably need the help of a bulldozer and front-end loader—an expensive job. If the area is reasonably small, you can tackle it with a shovel and rake and do it yourself in a few weeks.

Grading strips the topsoil from the land and leaves a subsoil base. The subsoil (after being bulldozed or raked to the desired depth) should be leveled and the topsoil should be replaced. Before you put down topsoil, any soil compacted from heavy equipment will need turning and churning because plants will not grow in hard clay, which prevents water from getting to the roots.

There are many kinds of topsoil. Get the best you can afford, as it pays off in lush, green plants that need little care, rather than weak ones that always need attention. Inspect topsoil before buying and purchase from a reputable supplier to be sure of its quality. Topsoil should be black, crumbly and porous. Topsoil from unreliable sources is often soil excavated from another nearby site and is full of sticks, stones and other debris. It is not mixed or screened. Topsoil is delivered to the site by truck and is dumped at the site. (See Chapter Two, The Service Area, about deliveries.) You must do your own shoveling and spreading.

GOOD SOIL MAKES THE DIFFERENCE

Earth or soil has two layers—topsoil and subsoil. The subsoil beneath the surface layer has been there for hundreds of years. It can be from a few inches deep to 20 inches (50.8 cm) below the surface. Topsoil is composed of small particles of disintegrated rock, minerals and decomposing organic matter; living organisms such as bacteria and fungi; and water, which holds the dissolved minerals, salts and air. Over the years most soils lose their mineral content and must be reworked and revitalized.

Inspect the physical conditions of the subsoil around your house while it is exposed. Once it is covered with topsoil you will never know what lies beneath until plants refuse to grow and then die. If the subsoil is claylike, it will hold water too long and cause sick, waterlogged plants. On the other hand, in sandy soils roots do not have a chance to absorb water. Now—not later—is the time to correct soil deficiencies.

It is difficult, but not impossible, to improve the conditions of clay soil. (Some plants do prefer moist or wet soils, but they are the exceptions.) Most clay soils will drain better if coarse sand and humus is mixed into them.

Sandy soil is easy to work with and warms up quickly in the spring. However, it does not retain moisture and many of the plant soluble foods will be lost through leaching. Add liberal quantities of organic matter, humus, peat moss and compost to improve a sandy soil.

All soil must be reasonably loose and porous; it must breathe. Air must reach microorganisms and chemicals in the soil, and water must penetrate it.

It is time to add topsoil only after subsoils have been corrected. Most nurseries will tell you that a thin layer of topsoil is all that you need to grow plants. Don't believe it unless you are a stellar gardener! You will need at least 4 inches (10.2 cm) of topsoil; 8 inches (20.3 cm) is better for lush trees and shrubs.

If the bulldozer is still available have the topsoil delivered immediately so that the operator can spread it for you. Otherwise, you must tediously transport the soil by wheelbarrow or bucket.

✿

Chapter Two

PLANNING THE
SMALL GARDEN

*E*very site is different and every garden plan is different. One of the joys of having your own yard is that you can design it to your own tastes. To begin to plan your property, it is wise to have a sketch on paper. First, make a plan of what you want the outdoor living space to do for you and what you can do for it to make it attractive.

Creating this plan is exciting. The arrangement you select and the plants you put into the ground—the entire picture is your very own. And in most parts of the country (without temperate all-year climate) it is a changing picture as seasons change. The plan you eventually select should be one that you can carry out over a period of years; it is not something to do in one season.

Laying out the garden involves the shapes and dimensions of the house and site, the functions and uses desired by the owners and the plants and structural materials to be used.

PLANNING ON PAPER

A general ground plan of the property does not have to be drawn to scale; it can be a sketch. Try to obtain a plot plan showing the site dimensions. (Your builder or contractor can give you one.) Using this as your guide, transpose the location of the house and boundary lines onto graph paper. Let each square represent a foot. Draw an outline of the house, put in steps, walks and driveways, and show existing trees and shrubs. Use basic landscape design symbols for each item (see Figure 2.1).

Mark high and low areas on the paper. Show where there is sunlight and shade, and indicate the north point of reference (see Figure 2.2). Make a written list of the things you want on your property—dining area, terrace, fountain or pool, flower bed, hedges and such absolutely essential things as walks, paths, driveways, garage and play and work areas.

Over the graph paper lay a sheet of tracing paper, keeping the list of things you want at your side. Sketch traffic patterns first on the tracing paper. Then draw in the rough sizes and shapes of objects you want outdoors (terrace, garden beds, trees and shrubs and whatever else is

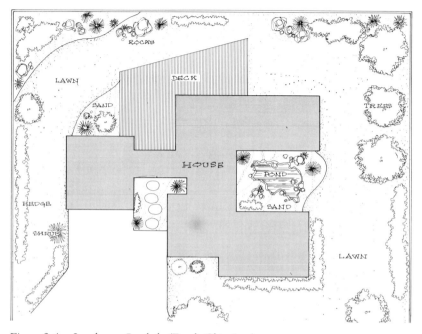

Figure 2.1—Landscape Symbols (Frank Chin Loy)

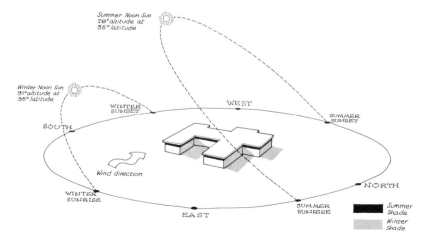

Figure 2.2—Sun Orientation Chart (Frank Chin Loy)

necessary). Now the irregularly drawn shapes should start to relate to each other. If you are not pleased with the layout, start over on a new sheet of tracing paper. Consider all things carefully, making several drafts before going on to a detailed plan.

Once a satisfactory rough sketch is done, a detailed design is necessary. Exactness counts now, so be sure to have the proper measurements of the house, lot, objects and existing plant material. Decide how much construction will be necessary in the garden—fences, screens, terraces, walls—and how much planting will be necessary.

SOME LANDSCAPING FUNDAMENTALS

To make full use of a small property, follow these fundamental rules:

1. Suit the design to the character of the house and site. Keep all elements in scale. Do not use large trees or shrubs for a small house or tiny plants for large house.

2. Create one or two features for eye interest—for example, a terrace, a small fountain or a lush area of flowers.

3. Do not overplant, but do put in enough plants to create an attractive setting in the second year. If you follow planting instructions for spacing plants from nurseries, it will take you four or five years to develop a handsome picture.

4. Strive for a harmonious garden plan in which all objects are related. Do this by repeating shapes and employing the same materials.

5. Consider ground cover instead of a lawn, which usually requires constant maintenance.

6. If there is a slope on the site, take advantage of it for terracing.

7. Plan your property so that it does not require constant upkeep.

THE OUTDOOR ROOM

A patio or a terrace, even a small one, can serve as a place for dining outdoors, growing plants or viewing, and should be near the house for convenience. It can be on the side of the house, in the front or, as in most cases, in the rear of the property where there is generally space and privacy. Remember that this secluded area is your quiet retreat.

The outdoor area does not have to be large, but it should be attractive and needs more care in planning than a large site. If possible, break up the property into several patios. Keep each one a sensible size and treat them individually. One can be small and charming; another can be more elaborate. The shape of the outdoor area also should be considered. Many patios are square or rectangular, but there is no set rule; there are circular, elliptical and free-form shapes. The site, the architecture of the house and personal tastes dictate the patio design.

At the end of this small garden is a quaint gazebo; the path to the structure is planted handsomely with a variety of flowers. (Photo by Luckhardt)

Almost any paving can be used as an outside floor. Tile and outdoor carpeting are sometimes popular, but they are more costly than brick or concrete block. Because there are so many pavings available, select your materials and designs carefully. (See Chapter Three.)

Although a patio may be detached from a house, when integrated with the house it offers advantages. The living area is extended beyond the walls, and the inside rooms seem larger. Used as an occasional dining room, set near the kitchen, during parties it can accommodate an overflow of guests.

The patio or terrace is the outdoor area where you and your family will spend the most time, so make it pleasant and private. It can become the most important living space of the home for many months of the year.

APPROACH TO THE HOUSE

The approach to the house, usually referred to as the front yard, often has been neglected, and yet it is here that a visitor receives his first impression of what is to come. Necessity often dictates an open front yard, but the small enclosed court or entry patio should not be ignored. The front of the house may be a better garden site than the rear when the following conditions are present:

1. A steep hill slopes down to the rear of the house.

2. The house is set back far from the front lot line.

3. Neighbors' windows overlook the rear.

4. The view from the front is good.

5. The sun/wind relationship is better in the front.

Enclosing the front of your property may seem unconventional; however, it is an old idea borrowed from English manor and Spanish country houses. The enclosed yard provides a pleasant and effective entrance through a private garden, and the overall setting for the house is greatly enhanced. Fences today are no longer massive and unsightly or expensive. There are many materials besides wood with which to make fences. Concrete blocks are available in many patterns and are easy to install; bricks are always charming, but a brick fence requires professional skill to build.

Once you decide on an entry court garden, consider the same principles of design and arrangement as for the rear area: privacy, the appearance of the area in relation to the house and the selection of proper plant materials placed strategically. In the front, landscaping becomes a setting for the house and a garden; it is a dual area. A large house demands specimen plants; for a smaller house, container plants are suitable as long as they are in scale with the architecture and in harmony with all other plantings.

THE SERVICE AREA

This area is often neglected, but it is the heart of the plan. Trash cans, clotheslines, tool sheds and the vegetable and cutting gardens are all part of the service region. Here too is the garage or carport and the driveway. Trucks will deliver building materials "tailgate," which means to your driveway only; moving and hauling takes time and hard work and is expensive if you have to hire someone to do it.

Try to screen trash or garbage cans from view; use sunken cans or a small box with a wooden top. If possible, keep the cans in the garage or perhaps at a small angle in the fence so that they are hidden. Even though garbage cans should be close to the kitchen so that there is a minimum of carrying, be sure to put them far enough from the house so that odors do not permeate the house or terrace.

Today, driveways and garages are a planning lesson in themselves; they must have design and spacing to be functional. Make

This small garden is useful and handsome; there is a potting area and the vertical arbor defines the space. Note the container plants and various vines to balance the vertical lines. (Photo by Matthew Barr)

driveways wide enough for vehicles, and definitely have a car turnaround; it is essential for owners and guests. Try not to have the driveway to the garage on a steep grade; excavate or fill it if possible to obtain greater safety. Never slope the driveway toward the house. If you do, rainwater will flow directly into the garage. It is a good idea to frame the driveway with shrubs, but be sure that you select low-growing ones so that they won't obscure the view of oncoming cars.

Make a carport at least 18 by 27 feet (5.5 x 8.2 m) with a hard-surfaced floor—concrete or asphalt. Allow a gentle slope for the roof so that water can run off easily. To prevent soil erosion around the carport, use gutters or downspouts from the roof into a drain line. Most carports are bare and look unsightly, so add some potted plants for charm. It takes but a few minutes to make this structure a handsome addition to the plan rather than an eyesore.

Since power tools and hand tools are necessary for the garden, and often storing and hauling them to the site is hard work, a utility shed should be near the garden area. These sheds should have doors that you can close. Commercial sheds can be purchased, or you can make your own.

If it is not possible to have a closed storage shed, try screening this utility area. Hedges and fences are enough protection if tools must be left outdoors. Of course, in the winter they will have to be stored in a closed area, such as the garage.

❧

Chapter Three

Surfacing for the Small Garden

Surfacing is an important part of planning a small property. Too often people put down a slab of concrete for a patio or terrace and then are disappointed when the outdoor living area is sterile and uninviting. The paved area must be a part of the total design and fit into the picture (see Figure 3.1).

PATIOS AND TERRACES

Today a patio or terrace is almost essential for the outdoor area. It can be an excavated place filled with gravel or stone, but more likely it will be an area that is paved for aesthetic reasons. The paving material can be brick or concrete, tile or flagstone, carpeting or precast slabs or patio blocks. Each has character, texture, usefulness and appeal; how you put it all together is what makes a garden attractive. Depending on the surfacing used, patterns can vary immeasurably. Remember that pavings are usually geometrically shaped—squares, rectangles, octagons—and pleasing patterns will create interest that lessens monotony and provides decorative accent. Blocks or bricks can be laid in infinite patterns, but keep the patterns simple and attractive; the overdesigned terrace floor can be as upsetting as the overpatterned living-room carpet. It will detract from, rather than enhance, the garden setting, so sketch several patterns before you start. Surfacing can add more charm and character for less money than plantings and other features. It also requires only an occasional washing rather than planting and garden maintenance.

Try to blend whatever type of material you select with the existing materials—in the house or the boundaries—and with

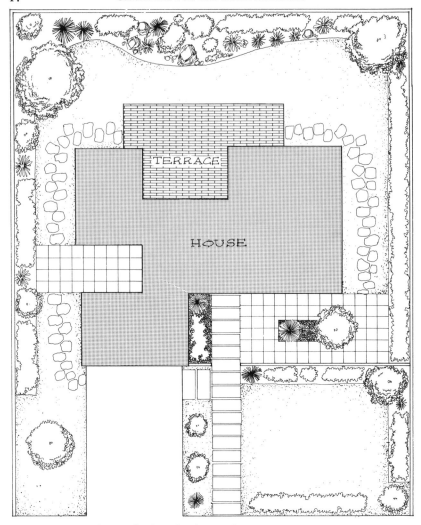

Figure 3.1—Garden Walks (Frank Chin Loy)

borders and plant containers. In other words, repeat the patterns or materials throughout the garden; this gives an illusion of space.

For economy and easy installation the square or rectangular patio is best. Curved paved areas are more costly and take more time to install because paving slabs and blocks must be cut.

The actual paving area depends on the house and lot size and how it is going to be used. For patios, make the area reasonably large so that it is usable (at least 14 by 20 (4.2 x 6 m) for an average home). The patio should, if possible, adjoin the living or dining room.

SURFACING MATERIALS

When you are considering the available paving materials, ask the following questions:

1. Will the surface level off smoothly for quick drainage?

2. Will the paving produce glare?

3. Will the paving be slippery when wet? (Concrete is.)

4. Does the material harmonize with the house and garden structures?

5. Can the floor be easily maintained?

6. Can the surfacing be laid at a reasonable cost?

7. Will the floor be weather-resistant?

8. Can you do some of the work yourself? (Some floors are easy to install; others need heavy equipment.)

PAVING MATERIALS

There are a number of different paving materials, each with its own benefits and drawbacks. All can be attractive additions to the small garden.

CONCRETE

Concrete makes a satisfactory patio floor, with some modifications. As mentioned, it needs design and thought. Developers have a habit of throwing down a slab of concrete against one house wall and calling it a patio. This large surface is rarely attractive, soon cracks and is slippery.

If you use concrete, divide the space into squares—6- to 8-foot (1.8- to 2.4-m) squares. Larger squares require reinforcing to prevent cracking. Filling between the squares is not necessary if you allow each one to set before laying the next one; however, for looks you might want to use wood strips between the concrete (see Figure 3.2). If the gray color of concrete is monotonous, use a coarse gravel aggregate in the concrete to eliminate the sterile look and add texture to the area.

BRICK

Brick has a natural look, is attractive outdoors and provides a nonglare, nonskid surface. It is easy to install and inexpensive, and

Large concrete aggregate squares make an attractive path in this garden; additional masonry is used to provide balance.

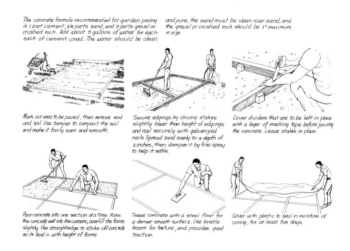

The concrete formula recommended for garden paving is 1 part cement, 2¼ parts sand, and 3 parts gravel or crushed rock. Add about 5 gallons of water for each sack of cement used. The water should be clean and pure, the sand must be clean river sand, and the gravel or crushed rock should be 1" maximum in size.

Mark out area to be paved, then remove sod and soil. Use tamper to compact the soil and make it fairly even and smooth.

Secure edgings by driving stakes slightly lower than height of edgings and nail securely with galvanized nails. Spread sand evenly to a depth of 2 inches, then dampen it by fine spray to help it settle.

Cover dividers that are to be left in place with a layer of masking tape before pouring the concrete. Leave stakes in place.

Pour concrete into one section at a time. Rake the concrete well into the corners, overfill the forms slightly. Use straightedge to strike-off concrete so its level is with height of forms.

Trowel concrete with a steel float for a denser smooth surface. Use bristle broom for texture, and provides good traction.

Cover with plastic to seal in moisture of curing, for at least five days.

Figure 3.2—Constructing a Concrete Patio (Frank Chin Loy)

comes in different patterns and colors. It can be used in combination with other hard flooring materials for a handsome effect. It is an ideal paving with but one drawback—when covered with water, frequently it becomes coated with algae and can be slippery.

Brick comes in a variety of earthy colors, rough or smooth surfaced, and glazed or unglazed. Different shapes are available (hexagonal and octagonal, for example), but they must be used with caution because shaped bricks require precise installation and manipulation of pattern.

The best patio bricks are smooth-surfaced or rough-textured common brick. Select hard-burned instead of green brick; it is dark

This small garden area is neatly defined with suitable paths; the tall dahlias provide necessary vertical accent. (Photo by Luckhardt)

red rather than the salmon color that indicates an underburned process and less durability. Used bricks are fine too if you can locate them, but often, because of their natural look, they are more expensive than new brick. Be sure the dealer has enough of the brick you select to complete the floor, for usually there are some dimensional variations and color differences in later brick purchases.

To save money, you can install a brick-on-sand paving (see Figure 3.3). It is not difficult, but does require patience. Mark out

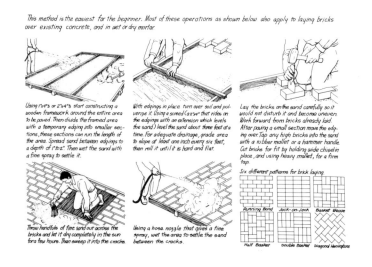

This method is the easiest for the beginner. Most of these operations as shown below also apply to laying bricks over existing concrete, and in wet or dry mortar.

Using 1"x4"'s or 2"x4"'s start constructing a wooden framework around the entire area to be paved. Then divide the framed area with a temporary edging into smaller sections, these sections can run the length of the area. Spread sand between edgings to a depth of 1" to 2". Then wet the sand with a fine spray to settle it.

With edgings in place turn over soil and pulverize it. Using a screed (a 2"x4" that rides on the edgings with an extension which levels the sand) level the sand about three feet at a time. For adequate drainage, grade area to slope at least one inch every six feet, then roll it until it is hard and flat.

Lay the bricks on the sand carefully so it would not disturb it and become uneven. Work forward from bricks already laid. After paving a small section move the edging over. Tap any high bricks into the sand with a rubber mallet or a hammer handle. Cut bricks for fit by holding wide chisel in place, and using heavy mallet, for a firm tap.

Throw handfuls of fine sand out across the bricks and let it dry completely in the sun for a few hours. Then sweep it into the cracks.

Using a hose nozzle that gives a fine spray, wet the area to settle the sand between the cracks.

Six different patterns for brick laying.

Running Bond   Jack-on-Jack   Basket Weave
Half Basket   Double Basket   Diagonal Herringbone

Figure 3.3—How to Set Bricks on Sand (Frank Chin Loy)

the site with string and stakes; then excavate, grade, and level the ground. Put in a perfectly level sand base of 3 inches (7.6 cm). (The floor will be wavy and visually distracting if the ground is not level.) Do the floor in sections, a small piece at a time, rather than trying to do the whole area in a day.

To cut bricks, use a cold chisel or a brick hammer. Cut a groove along one side of the brick and give it a sharp, severing blow. Smooth uneven edges of the brick by rubbing them with another brick.

On the 3-inch (7.6-cm) sand base set the bricks in place as closely together as possible, and check each row with a level. Dust sand into the cracks. Slope the floor away from the house at an incline of 1 inch (2.5 cm) per 6 feet (1.8 m) of paving.

Bricks can be laid in herringbone, basketweave, running-bond, soldier-course, and stretcher-bond patterns, or combine them with grass squares or cinders in endless designs. In large areas use the herringbone pattern; smaller patios look best with a running-bond or basketweave pattern. For very large areas use redwood or cedar grids between the bricks for a handsome effect.

Brick can be set in mortar, but this is usually a job for a professional bricklayer.

PRECAST SLABS

Precast slabs are very popular and come in a variety of colors and sizes. They are inexpensive and easy to install, and provide a nonslip durable surface. The slabs are available in 1 1/2-inch (3.8-cm) and 2-inch (5-cm) thicknesses.

Be wary of the very colorful slabs; when they are mixed with other landscape colors, the result often is too garish. Test the color of the slab when both wet and dry, for there is quite a difference.

Slabs can be installed in many patterns. Mix sizes for a random block effect or use one size or try some of the hexagonal or circular shapes. Remember that the jointing has to be done with precision care.

Excavate enough to allow for a 3-inch (7.6-cm) sand base and the thickness of the concrete block. The blocks can be laid on the sand base or on concrete and joined together with mortar for more durability. You can butt-joint the blocks by putting them in place as closely together as possible and filling the interstices with mortar. Or you can use a dry mix filling (brush a dry sand and cement mixture at the rate of five to one between the joints when the slabs are laid). Spray with water afterward and allow to set.

Precast slabs of concrete aggregate panels are also available; install in the same manner.

FLAGSTONE

Flagstone is either square or rectangular and gives a rich lifetime surface. The irregularity of the material is part of its charm, and its colors—buff, brownish red and gray—add warmth to the patio. Flagstone is hard, stratified stone (shale, slate or marble) split into flat pieces that can be installed dry or in mortar. For masonry, use 1-inch-thick (2.5-cm-thick) stone; for dry laying, use 1 1/2-inch-thick (3.8-cm-thick) stone.

If the ground is well drained and level, flagstones can be installed directly on it. (They will shift somewhat in very cold weather, but will remain in place.) For a sturdier and better floor, set the flagstones in sand; a 2-inch (5-cm) bed is fine. Firmly place the flagstones over the entire surface and make sure that they are really in place, so that no listing will occur. Fill in the joints with soil that is flush with the surface of the stones, and wet it down thoroughly. For a permanent paving, set flags on a 3-inch (7.6-cm) concrete bed.

INDOOR-OUTDOOR CARPETING

Indoor-outdoor carpeting is made in easy-to-install blocks of various sizes and colors. However, it can and does stain, and after a while it deteriorates and has to be replaced. Furthermore, although it looks good in the home, it generally looks odd when used outdoors. It is useful, though, around pools because it provides a nonskid, soft surface. It can also be used effectively for small patio areas, but for large expanses hard-surfacing looks better, lasts longer and needs little maintenance.

WALKS AND STEPS

Walks and paths are necessary so that you can move around your garden with ease. Brick, precast stone slabs, wood rounds, cinder, gravel and fir bark are all good materials for paths, but it is important to use them in harmony with the garden plan. For instance, in a woodsy setting, wood rounds or fir bark add warmth and charm; concrete would be out of place. While it is essential to have paths, either make them as unobtrusive as possible or make them an integral part of the plan. To do this, repeat the pattern and material elsewhere in the garden so the plan is coordinated.

A path to the house is another garden necessity; it must be direct, well paved and wide enough for two people to walk side by side. A 6-foot (1.8-m) width is generally suitable. A wide, shallow step in front of the door adds charm to the scene and is a place for container plants in summer.

While a curved path is certainly feasible and adds grace to the plan, a straight walk is acceptable too. Any patio surfacing—brick, tile, concrete blocks—can also be used for walks. Install brick or concrete blocks on a level bed of sand or cinders to allow water to seep through. Use a 3-inch (7.6-cm) bed of cinders and then add a 1-inch (2.5-cm) layer of sand. Unless bricks are installed as closely together as they can be, they will become loose. With whatever paving you use, allow for adequate draining underneath the surface.

Steps are dramatic accents in a garden and should be used more. They can break the monotony of a large site, and there are infinite arrangements. They may be irregular with various angles and turns and interestingly shaped islands. A wide tread and a short rise are best for garden steps; a 15-inch (38.1-cm) tread with a rise of about 5 to 6 inches (12.7 to 15.2 cm) is a good average.

Try to avoid too many steps in one area; it is best to use two or three of them where a change of levels is necessary and repeat the arrangement later.

Chapter Four

TRELLIS AND ESPALIER GARDENING

Growing plants vertically rather than horizontally enables you to maintain a garden in limited space. By growing vegetables, fruit trees, vines, berries or whatever on wooden trellises (also called lattices), you can enjoy the delights of gardening as well as provide decorative accent for your outdoor areas. Trellises can be installed on a back porch, in a small entryway, against a patio wall or alongside a garage—anywhere you want to increase your growing area (see Figures 4.1a and 4.1b). And with an overhead canopy, a trellis can become a beautiful hanging garden. Vegetables and vines have to be tied to and then trained on trellises at first, but in a short time plants grow on their own, with only occasional training.

Trellises offer other pluses as well. First, vertical growing eliminates undue stooping and bending. You can walk around your garden and tend plants at waist level and eye level rather than having to kneel on the ground or stoop over. Also, you can see plants better in a standing position. Second, trellis gardening helps plants because air is able to

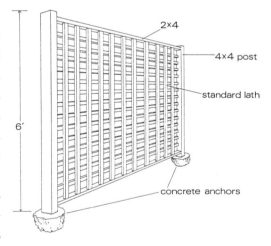

Figure 4.1a—Free-Standing Trellis (Michael Valdez)

reach all parts of the plant. Plants with good air circulation grow better. Finally, growing plants vertically eliminates many insects because insects tend to crawl horizontally.

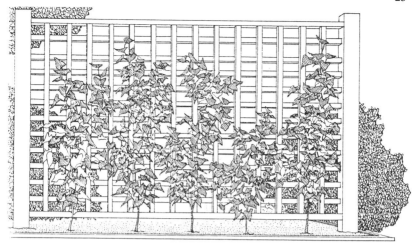

Figure 4.1b—Free-Standing Trellis (Michael Valdez)

In small areas growing plants against a wall (espalier) is a good idea and gives the garden a somewhat unique look. (Photo by Matthew Barr)

DECORATIVE EFFECT

A trellis provides vertical garden interest, which is a good design aspect—you balance horizontal lines with vertical ones. To maintain the good looks of a trellis, do not overdo the plants or the result will be a tangled mess. You want to create a light and graceful look.

TRELLISING GUIDELINES

Follow these six guidelines to achieve a harmonious effect:

1. Arrange laths so plants are adequately supported. Be sure laths are close enough to permit the securing of small shoots.

2. In shady and secluded areas, create intimate nooks by using close-patterned trellises.

3. Install trellises in sections, with posts at intervals when spanning a distance. This technique provides vertical accent in long horizontal distances that have no breaks.

4. Use trellising with closely spaced laths for small-growing plants with small leaves.

5. If there is an interesting view on the other side of the trellis, space strips far apart to achieve a peek-through look, which is very handsome.

6. If training plants against a flat surface (espaliering), be sure the trellis has enough space, about 4 to 6 inches (10.2 to 15.2 cm), between laths.

ESPALIERS

To grow fruit in small spaces, espalier the trees on trellises. With this method, in a space of 20 feet (6 m), you can grow four dwarf fruit trees against a fence. Espaliering is training plants to grow flat against a surface, with 4 to 6 inches (10.2 to 15.2 cm) of air space behind plants. The plants are then trimmed to a desired shape. Espaliered plants take time to grow and cover an area; it is easier to plant an espalier already started (such plants are sold at nurseries).

Formal espalier patterns are not now as popular as informal or free-form espaliers (see Figure 4.2), which do not require as much trimming and training as the formal ones. Among the symmetrical formal patterns (see figure 4.3) are *double horizontal cordon* (center shoot with two horizontal branches), *vertical U shape* and *double and triple U shapes* (vertical stem on each side of a central trunk), *palmette verrier* (candelabra pattern), *palmette oblique* (branches trained in a fan shape), *horizontal T* (multiple horizontal cordon with several horizontals on each side of a vertical trunk), *Belgian fence* (diamond pattern) and *arcure* (series of connecting arcs). Fasten plant stems to surfaces with special nails or copper wire.

Grow espalier fruit trees either in containers or in the ground, in a well-drained, rich soil. Do *not* fertilize espaliers; overfed plants are impossible to keep trained to the desired shape.

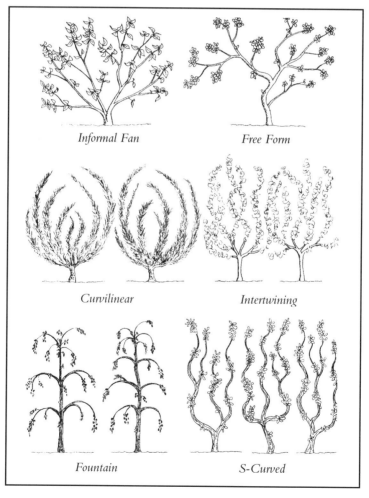

Figure 4.2—Informal Espalier (Heidi L. Herndon)

FRUIT TREE CONSIDERATIONS

Select trees for the season you want—fruit trees bear at different times of the year. Also consider bearing time—apples and pears bear in four to six years; plums, cherries, and peaches bear in about four years. Fruit trees come in standard or dwarf sizes, in many varieties. Be sure the fruit trees you buy are hardy enough to stand your area's coldest winter and hottest summer.

Many fruit trees are self-sterile. In other words, they will bear a crop only if blossoming plants are nearby, to supply pollen. Certain fruit trees are self-pollinating or fruiting.

Buy one- or two-year-old trees from local nurseries. The nursery personnel can tell you about bearing seasons and time, trees

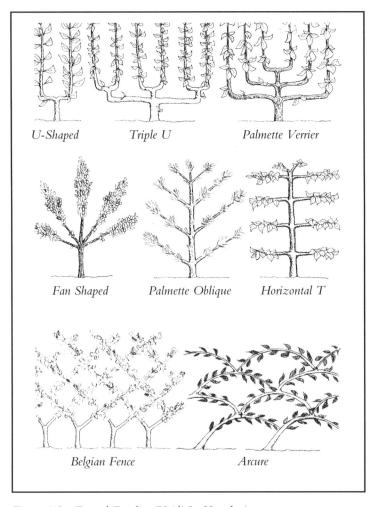

Figure 4.3—Formal Espalier (Heidi L. Herndon)

good for your area and whether trees are self-sterile or self-pollinating. Stone fruits are usually one year old; apples and pears are usually two years old. Trees should be stocky and branching, for balance.

Plant trees as soon as possible, before hot sun kills them. If you cannot plant right away, temporarily plant (heel in) the trees. In a shallow trench wide enough to receive tree roots, set plants on their sides and cover the roots with soil and then water them. Try to keep new trees out of the hot sun and high winds.

When you are ready to plant, be sure the soil is friable and workable with air in it (porous). Fruit trees will not make it in dry, sandy soil or hard clay soil. Planting holes should be deep enough so you can set the plants in at the depth they were at the nursery and wide enough to hold roots without crowding.

Be sure the planting area is in the sun. Plant trees about 10 to 15 feet (3 to 4.5 m) apart, in fall or spring, when the land is warm. Pack the soil in place firmly but not tightly and water plants thoroughly. Again, do *not* feed fruit trees. However, do give newly planted trees an application of B-12 to help them recover from transplanting.

The trunk of the fruit tree should be 12 to 18 inches (30.4 to 45.7 cm) from the base of the trellis. *Sparsely* prune young trees. Tie branches to the trellis firmly enough to keep branches flat. As the trees grow, increase trimming and tieing to establish the desired espalier pattern.

Attach the trellis to a wall or support with wire or a trellis support gadget (at nurseries). In a masonry wall, place raw plugs in the mortared joints, and insert screw eyes. (Use a carbide drill to make holes in any masonry.)

CARE

Give your fruit trees good soil, water, sun and protection from insects. Only when trees are actively growing can you start feeding with a weak solution of fruit tree fertilizer (at nurseries). Remember that too much fertilizer can harm trees. If leaves become yellow, the soil may not contain enough nutrients, especially iron, so add iron chelate to it. Wilted leaves often indicate that water is not reaching the roots or insects are present. You can use a dormant oil spray in early spring to get rid of bugs. Your Agricultural

Extension Service (see Appendix) can give you information about fruit tree diseases and preventatives.

PRUNING

A plant dormant before new foliage has started in spring can be heavily pruned. With mature plants, start shaping them *after* they flower. You can lightly prune every month during the growing season. Pruning plants in late summer encourages new growth that will not have time to mature before cold weather sets in.

Prune the roots of your espaliers only if plants are growing larger than you want for their location. Prune roots in early spring to cut off feeder roots and curtail rampant growth. To prune roots, spade out the ground 3 to 4 feet (.9 to 1.2 m) from the base of the plants.

Chapter Five

DRIP-SYSTEM
WATERING

*A*ll plants need water to survive. However, too much water can be just as damaging to plants as too little—how can you be sure you are watering correctly? Hoses and sprinklers and even underground sprinklers waste water because they supply more water to the ground than to roots, unlike drip systems, which slowly supply plant roots with the necessary amount of water.

When you water plants with a hose, the water can take up to ninety minutes to penetrate 24 inches (61 cm) into the soil (see Table 5.1). Thus you have to hose almost all day for moisture to reach deep into the soil to the roots. Remember, water from a hose moves laterally in the soil rather than fanning out. And hose watering is spotty because pockets of wet and dry soil result. Those roots that do not get enough or any water will grow in other directions to seek moisture, thus sapping the strength from plants.

Table 5.1—Time for Water to Penetrate Soils			
	Soil Type		
Soil Depth	Coarse Sand	Sandy Loam	Clay Loam
12 inches (30.4 cm)	15 min.	30 min.	60 min.
24 inches (61 cm)		60 min.	90 min.
30 inches (76.2 cm)	40 min.	90 min.	
48 inches (122 cm)	60 min.		

Other problems with hoses are kinking, cracking or breaking in cold weather, and eventual loss of resiliency. Rubber hoses do not crack, but they are expensive ($30 to $50).

Sprinklers oscillate water, pulsate water, arc water or spew water in all directions—everything but water plants correctly.

Underground sprinklers operate with or without a switch and are regulated by a time clock. Portable sprinklers deliver water to an area within only a 7- to 9-foot (2.1- to 2.7-m) radius. Water falls away from plants rather than on them. Most of the water evaporates in the air and runs off the surface of the soil, especially if the soil is hard clay. If you rearrange your plantings, you must revamp the underground system or move the portable sprinklers. Sprinklers also frequently break down. Another disadvantage is that within a sprinkler the water pressure fluctuates, thus erratically supplying moisture to plants.

PLANNING A DRIP SYSTEM

A drip system can take on several forms with several different types of emitters (see Figures 5.1 and 5.2). It can be either above or below ground and laid out with a spur line or in a channel pattern. First you should consider soil texture, the types of plants you are growing and various water factors.

Texture of the Soil. Soil texture (tilth) affects how you water plants. Water runs through sandy soils quickly to reach plant roots, but water has a tough time penetrating clay soil. (Good soil feels mealy, like a well-done baked potato.) A standard emitter setup is sufficient for a fairly porous soil, but more emitters are necessary in planting areas with hard soil. Rototilling clay soil will ensure that the soil is porous enough to allow water to run through it.

Plants Grown. Vegetables and flowers need larger amounts of water more often than shrubs and trees. Thus a garden of only evergreens needs less water than a flower or vegetable garden.

Water. You must consider the quality and availability of water in your area. In areas of limited water or saline water supply, a drip system is essential. Saline water applied through hoses and sprinklers is too salty and can kill plants, but drip systems administer small amounts of water slowly, diluting the salt content to a safe level.

Your next step is to sketch the garden area on graph paper. Measure off the area and then draw in existing plants, using different shapes for shrubs, trees, flowers and so on. Whether you supply drip water to all areas of the garden depends on the area's size. In the average garden of 20 by 40 feet (6 x 12.2 m) you can incorporate a total drip-system setup. You can start with a small system and then add to it later. (Grasses and seeded areas need soaker rather than emitter drip systems.)

After you map out the existing plants, draw in the drip systems you will need—a row pattern for vegetables and flowers, a point (grid) pattern in another area. Selection of the systems depend on the number of plants and the distance between them. Now determine where to place hoses and install emitters.

WATERING CONSIDERATIONS

If you dislike the conspicuous appearance of hoses and pipes on the soil, consider the more expensive method of locating them underground. However, remember that as they grow, plants will cover aboveground hoses and pipes.

You must consider the wet zone (the area around the roots of the plant) when determining how much and when to water. The size and shape of the wet zone varies according to (1) the type of soil, (2) the rate at which plants take moisture from the soil in regard to the number of emitters used and (3) the rate at which the emitters discharge water.

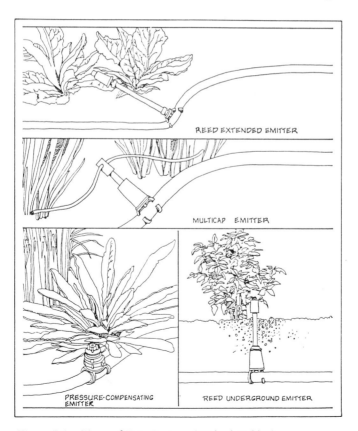

REED EXTENDED EMITTER

MULTICAP EMITTER

PRESSURE-COMPENSATING EMITTER

REED UNDERGROUND EMITTER

Figure 5.1—Types of Drip Systems (Michael Valdez)

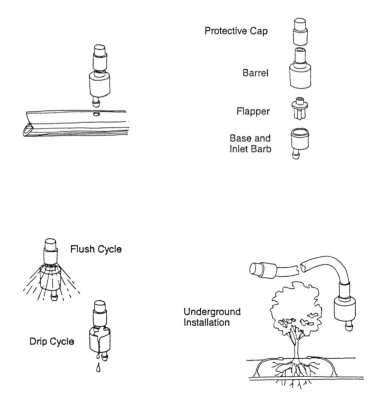

Figure 5.2—Component Parts of Drip Systems (Michael Valdez)

Gravity moves water downward, and capillary action spreads it in all directions. Because the capillary forces are stronger than gravitational ones in fine soil, the wet zone is circular. Coarse soil does not retain water very long, so the wet zone is elliptical.

Plants should be watered slowly so that they can absorb water and water will not run off. To avoid runoff and ponding, stop the water for a while and then turn it on again one to sixteen hours later. (If the time elapsed is more than sixteen hours, the number of emitters has to be increased.)

GENERAL LAYOUT

A good general garden plan consists of flowers in borders and beds and ornamental shrubs and trees as background, with a lawn or a patio in the center. Ideal for this layout is a perimeter system, with spur lines and emitters coming off the main hose line of standard 1/4-inch (.6-cm) hose (40 feet [12.2 m] for a 20-by-30-foot [6-x-9.1-m] garden). Most of the plants here are tall, so the line is set aboveground, with about twelve emitters near specific plants.

In a cutting garden, install the drip system in a U shape, with hoses parallel to the rows of plants. This is an easy system to lay out. A U pattern can also be used in a vegetable garden, although a grid pattern works equally well. Because vegetables require much water, the emitters should be spaced more closely than those in an ornamental garden.

Vegetable/Fruit Gardens. Vegetable gardens demand rich and porous soil. A drip system will save you time and ensure fewer weeds. Although the drip system costs more than hoses or sprinklers, you will get much more produce than with conventional watering, and the produce will taste much better.

Flower Gardens. In a flower garden you can put in a small drip system; nature (rain) will do the rest. Two drip kits (about $40) will supply moisture for the average flower garden.

Container Gardens. In a container garden, the lines must be run right into the containers. Soil in containers dries out much faster than soil in the ground, but with a drip system, container plants continuously receive a slow trickle of water and thus grow rapidly.

If you cannot attach the emitter for a single container overhead to a post or some other support you will have to resort to conventional watering methods. (I secure my 4- to 6-foot-long [1.2- to 1.8-cm-long] planter boxes to a wooden fence.)

Hillside Gardens. With ordinary watering, water runs off plants in hillside gardens, but drip systems feed water *slowly*, thus reducing runoff. Lay out the system in parallel rows spaced every 24 (61 cm) inches. Use pressure-compensating emitters so the water is distributed evenly to all plants.

Trees and Shrubs. With trees and shrubs, the initial layout is most important. Use the point system to install emitters close to shrubs and trees. A drip system will ensure beautiful greenery for years.

Lawns. Most lawns require intensive watering and upkeep. But underground drip soaker systems eliminate sprinkler heads and enable you to walk on the lawn while it is being watered. It is best to install the system before you plant a new lawn.

Underground soaker watering also saves you water and time (the system works at below normal water pressure). You can use black plastic tubing or PVC (polyvinylchloride) tubing. The black tubing, 8 mm thick, is really a tube within a tube. Water is dispersed through holes spaced 4 to 12 inches (10.2 to 30.4 cm) apart on the tube. The PVC tubing is flexible.

To install either the black or PVC tubing, lay the tubing in trenches then backfill and seed or plug the trenches. The system must have an in-line filtering unit that prevents clogging. Use a pressure regulator (15 pounds per square inch) or inexpensive flow-control fittings with black

This soaking hose provides slow moisture to plant roots and is a water saver. (Photo by Michael Jay)

tubing. A flow-control valve will work with PVC tubing. (All these hardware items are available from drip system suppliers.)

The new lawn needs daily hand watering until the grass grows to about 2 to 4 inches (5 to 10.2 cm), at which time you can begin using the watering system.

Chapter Six

PLANT MATERIALS AND HOW TO USE THEM

We are all familiar with shrubs and trees, but do we really know how to use them in the garden design? Each plant has a particular shape and quality; when you look at a tree, think of it as a design element rather than as a trunk with branches, and think of flowers as color and texture.

A sculptural tree is the focal point of this deck garden; it provides a handsome effect for the small area. (Photo courtesy California Redwood Association)

SHRUBS AND TREES

Trees and shrubs are the permanent framework of the garden, whether in boxes or tubs or in the ground. Once in place, they are part of the total picture for many years. They are divided into two groups: deciduous trees, which lose their leaves annually, and evergreen trees, which retain their leaves. There are two kinds of evergreens: the needle-leaved, cone-bearing shrubs and trees (conifers)—cedar, pine, spruce—and such broad-leaved evergreens as laurel and camellias. Because they hold color year round, evergreens are extremely popular.

There is a wide variation in foliage—the tiny leaves of heather, the bold leaves of evergreen magnolias, the large leaves of rhododendrons and so forth. Use plants in terms of the texture and pattern of their foliage when planning the garden.

Deciduous plants are mostly used in cold climates and temperate zones because they add the needed interest of seasonal change and are indispensable displays when in bloom. Because deciduous plants shed their leaves in the winter, however, a garden of them has an airy structure and lacks mass and strength, so one should use evergreens with them.

A plant's natural character is important in the overall plan; some grow in the shade and moisture and are dark green and lush. Others, such as desert plants, are generally pale green and sterile in appearance. Thus, try to approximate the natural growing conditions of garden plants so that they will be easy to maintain and look as if they belong to the scene. Trees are accents and form the garden's framework with shrubs massed around them. Perennials, annuals, biennials and bulbs provide seasonal color and contrast.

Deciduous trees seem difficult to place in the landscape unless you think of them without their leaves. Then the line pattern of the branches can be used effectively. Some trees, like the weeping willows with their pendant branches, are good for vertical accents because they carry the eye downward. Learn the architectural qualities of trees—columnar, mushroom-topped, fan-shaped, canopy—and use them accordingly to create a balanced design. Imagine the pattern of the tree against a winter sky and use the line of the tree—vertical, horizontal, pendant—to tie the landscape plan together.

The coniferous evergreens are strong and dark and add contrast. Do not use too many, for they break up a garden plan and will give a crowded appearance on a small property. Evergreens generally have clearly defined trunks; they frequently are effective as foundation plantings or are placed near a building.

Broad-leaved evergreen shrubs are lovely in bloom, but select them for foliage because they bloom only about one month of the year. The leaves and branches give a definite pattern to the entire textured mass. Some have big, bold leaves and others bear delicate lacy foliage. Pay attention to the related sequence of foliage as you place plants. A large-leaved shrub needs a medium-leaved one next to it, followed by a small-leaved shrub and ending with a tiny-leaved variety. Build up or down in relation to the leaf size—small, medium or large—to achieve the rhythm that is part of a lovely garden. A stand of any one shrub is usually monotonous and

Trees and shrubs provide the basic scenic components in this small courtyard garden; a small pool adds the crowning accent. (Photo by Matthew Barr)

overpowering. For an effective picture use shrubs with reference to leaf gradations.

Deciduous shrubs generally have somewhat soft, delicate foliage and are excellent behind perennials and annuals. Their leaves are akin to the soft texture of their flowers. When possible, use broad-leaved evergreens with their strong patterns and textures behind deciduous shrubs so that there is a gradual change of textures as the eye views the scene. There is no rough break or jarring transition, but rather smooth flow of plant material.

Shrubs for the Small Property

Botanical and Common Name	Type	Approx. Height	Minimum Night Temp.	Remarks
Abelia grandiflora (glossy abelia)	SE	5 ft (1.5 m)	−10° to −5°F (−23° to −20°C)	Free-flowering
Abeliophyllum distichum (Korean white forsythia)	D	3 to 4 ft (.9 to 1.2 m)	−10° to −5°F (−23° to −20°C)	Prune after bloom
Amelanchier canadensis (shadblow serviceberry)	D	30 ft (9.1 m)	−20° to −10°F (−29° to −23°C)	Slow grower
A. grandiflora (pink serviceberry)	D	25 ft (7.6 m)	−20° to −10°F (−29° to −23°C)	Large flowers
Andromeda polifolia (bog rosemary)	E	1 to 2 ft (.3 to .6 m)	−50° to −35°F (−45° to −37°C)	Likes moist locations
Arbutus unedo (strawberry tree)	E	10 to 20 ft (3 to 6 m)	10° to 20°F (−12° to −7°)	Does not like alkaline soil
Arctostaphylos manzanita (Parry manzanita)	E	6 to 20 ft (1.8 to 6 m)	5° to 10°F (−15° to −12°C)	Branching habit
A. uva-ursi (bearberry)	E	Groundcover	−50° to −35°F (−45° to −37°C)	Grows in any soil
Aucuba japonica (Japanese aucuba)	E	15 ft (4.5 m)	5° to 10°F (−15° to −12°C)	Good for shady places
Berberis koreana (Korean barberry)	D/E	2 to 10 ft (.6 to 3 m)	−10° to −5°F (−23° to −20°C)	Outstanding colors; red berries
B. thunbergii (Japanese barberry)	D/E	7 ft (2.1 m)	−10° to 5°F (−23° to −15°C)	Grows in any soil

Botanical and Common Name	Type	Approx. Height	Minimum Night Temp.	Remarks
Buddleia alternifolia (fountain buddleia)	D	12 ft (3.7 m)	–10° to –5°F (–23° to –20°C)	Graceful; branching
B. davidii (butterfly bush)	D/SE	15 ft (4.5 m)	–10° to –5°F (–23° to –20°C)	Many varieties
Buxus microphylla Japonica (Japanese boxwood)	E	4 ft (1.2 m)	–10° to –5°F (–23° to –20°C)	Low and compact
B. microphylla koreana (Korean boxwood)	E	6 to 10 ft (1.8 to 3 m)	–20° to –10°F (–29° to –23°C)	Hardiest; foliage turns brown in winter
B. sempervirens (common boxwood)	E	20 ft (6 m)	–10° to –5°F (–23° to –20°C)	Many varieties
Callistemon citrinus (Crimson bottlebrush)	E	25 ft (7.6 m)	20° to 30°F (–7° to –1°C)	Lovely flowers
Calluna vulgaris (Scotch heather)	E	15 ft (4.5 m)	–20° to –10°F (–29° to –23°C)	Bright color and foliage
Carissa grandiflora (natal plum)	E	15 ft (4.5 m)	20° to 30°F (–7° to –1°C)	Spiny; branching
Carpenteria californica (California mock orange)	E	8 ft (2.4 m)	5° to 20°F (–15° to –7°C)	Showy shrub
Ceanothus americanus (New Jersey tea)	E	3 ft (.9 m)	–20° to –10°F (–29° to –23°C)	For poor soil
Ceanothus ovatus (redroot)	E	3 ft (.9 m)	–20° to –10°F (–29° to –23°C)	Upright grower
Ceanothus thyrsiflorus (blueblossom)	E	30 ft (9.1 m)	–20° to –10°F (–29° to –23°C)	Grows in sandy soil
Chaenomeles speciosa (Japanese quince)	D	6 ft (1.8 m)	–20° to –10°F (–29° to –23°C)	Lovely flowers
C. superba (flowering quince)	D	6 ft (1.8 m)	–20° to –10°F (–29° to –23°C)	Fine hybrid
Clerodendrum trichotomum (glory-bower)	E	10 ft (3 m)	20° to 30°F (–7° to –1°C)	White flowers
Clethra alnifolia (summer-sweet)	D	9 ft (2.7 m)	–35° to –20°F (–37° to –29°C)	Fragrant summer bloom
Cornus alba 'Sibirica' (Siberian dogwood)	D	10 ft (3 m)	–50° to –35°F (–45° to –37°C)	Spectacular autumn color

Botanical and Common Name	Type	Approx. Height	Minimum Night Temp.	Remarks
C. mas (Cornelian cherry)	D	18 ft (5.5 m)	−20° to −5°F (−29° to −20°C)	Early blooming
Daphne odora (fragrant daphne)	D/E	4 to 6 ft (1.2 to 1.8 m)	5° to 10°F (−15° to −12°C)	Fragrant blossoms
Elaeagnus angustifolia (Russian olive)	D	20 ft (6 m)	−50° to −35°F (−45° to −37°C)	Fragrant flowers
E. multiflora (cherry elaeagnus)	D/E	9 ft (2.7 m)	−20° to −10°F (−29° to −23°C)	Bright red fruit
E. pungens (silverberry)	D/E	12 ft (3.7 m)	5° to 10°F (−15° to −12°C)	Vigorous grower
Enkianthus campanulatus (redvein enkianthus)	D	30 ft (9.1 m)	−20° to −10°F (−29° to −23°C)	Red autumn color
E. perulatus (Japanese enkianthus)	D	6 ft (1.8 m)	−10° to −5°F (−23° to −20°C)	Red autumn color
Erica canaliculata (Christmas heather)	E	6 ft (1.8 m)	20° to 30°F (−7° to −1°C)	Pink-purple flower
Eugenia uniflora (Surinam cherry)	E	10 to 15 ft (3 to 4.5 m)	20° to 30°F (−7° to −1°C)	White, fragrant flowers
Euonymus alata (winged euonymus)	D	9 ft (2.7 m)	−35° to −20°F (−37° to −29°C)	Sturdy; easily grown
E. japonica (evergreen euonymus)	E	15 ft (4.5 m)	10° to 20°F (−12° to −7°C)	Splendid foliage
E. latifolia (Algerian euonymus)	D	20 ft (6 m)	−10° to −5°F (−23° to −20°C)	Vigorous grower
E. sanguineas (Chinese euonymus)	D	20 ft (6 m)	−10° to −5°F (−23° to −20°C)	Best deciduous
Fatsia japonica (Japanese aralia)	E	15 ft (4.5 m)	5° to 10°F (−15° to −12°C)	Handsome foliage
Forsythia intermedia (border forsythia)	D	2 to 9 ft (.6 to 2.7 m)	−20° to −5°F (−29° to −20°C)	Deep yellow flowers
F. ovata (early forsythia)	D	8 ft (2.4 m)	−20° to −10°F (−29° to −23°C)	Earliest bloom and hardiest
Fothergilla major (large fothergilla)	D	9 ft (2.7 m)	−10° to −5°F (−23° to −20°C)	Good flowers and autumn color
Fuchsia magellanica (Magellan fuchsia)	D	3 ft (.9 m)	−10° to 5°F (−23° to −15°C)	Floriferous

Botanical and Common Name	Type	Approx. Height	Minimum Night Temp.	Remarks
Gardenia jasminoides (Cape jasmine)	E	4 to 6 ft (1.2 to 1.8 m)	10° to 30°F (−12° to −1°C)	Fragrant
Gaultheria shallon (salal)	E	5 ft (1.5 m)	−10° to −5°F (−23° to −20°C)	Sun or shade
G. veitchiana (veitch wintergreen)	E	3 ft (.9 m)	5° to 10°F (−15° to −12°C)	White or pink, bell-shaped flowers
Hamamelis mollis (Chinese witch hazel)	D	30 ft (9.1 m)	−10° to −5°F (−23° to −20°C)	Very fragrant flowers
H. vernalis (spring witch hazel)	D	10 ft (3 m)	−10° to −5°F (−23° to −20°C)	Early spring blooms
Hibiscus rosa-sinensis (Chinese hibiscus)	E	30 ft (9.1 m)	20° to 30°F (−7° to −1°C)	Stellar flower
H. syriacus (shrub althaea)	D	15 ft (4.5 m)	−10° to −5°F (−23° to −20°C)	Many varieties
Hydrangea arborescens 'Grandiflora' (hills-of-snow)	D	3 ft (.9 m)	−20° to −10°F (−29° to −23°C)	Easy culture
Hypericum densiflorum (dense hypericum)	D/SE	6 ft (1.8 m)	−10° to −5°F (−23° to −20°C)	Finely textured foliage
H. prolificum (broombrush)	S/SE	3 ft (.9 m)	−20° to −10°F (−29° to −23°C)	Very shrubby
Ilex cornuta (Chinese holly)	E	9 ft (2.7 m)	5° to 10°F (−15° to −12°C)	Bright berries; lustrous foliage
I. crenata (Japanese holly)	E	20 ft (6 m)	−5° to 5°F (−20° to −15°C)	Another good holly
Jasminum grandiflorum (Spanish jasmine)	SE/D	10 to 15 ft (3 to 4.5 m)	20° to 30°F (−7° to −1°C)	Blooms all summer
J. nudiflorum (winter jasmine)	D	15 ft (4.5 m)	−10° to −5°F (−23° to −20°C)	Viny shrub; not fragrant
J. officinale (white jasmine)	SE/D	30 ft (9.1 m)	5° to 10°F (−15° to −12°C)	Tall-growing
Juniperus chinensis 'Pfitzeriana' (Pfitzer juniper)	E	10 ft (3 m)	−20° to −10°F (−29° to −23°C)	Popular juniper
J. communis (common juniper)	E	30 ft (9.1 m)	−50° to −35°F (−45° to −37°C)	Many varieties
Kalmia angustifolia (sheep laurel)	E	3 ft (.9 m)	−50° to −35°F (−45° to −37°C)	Needs acid soil

Botanical and Common Name	Type	Approx. Height	Minimum Night Temp.	Remarks
K. latifolia (mountain laurel)	E	30 ft (9.1 m)	−20° to −10°F (−29° to −23°C)	Amenable grower
Kerria japonica (Japanese rose)	D	4 to 6 ft (1.2 to 1.8 m)	−20° to −10°F (−29° to −23°C)	Bright yellow flowers
Kolkwitzia amabilis (beautybush)	D	10 ft (3 m)	−20° to −10°F (−29° to −23°C)	Has many uses
Lagerstroemia indica (crape myrtle)	D	20 ft (6 m)	5° to 10°F (−15° to −12°C)	Popular summer bloom
Laurus nobilis (sweet bay)	E	30 ft (9.1 m)	−5° to 5°F (−20° to −15°C)	Tough plant
Leptospermum scoparium (tea tree)	E	6 to 20 ft (1.8 to 6 m)	20° to 30°F (−7° to −1°C)	Ground cover and shrubs
Ligustrum amurense (Amur privet)	D/E	6 to 30 ft (1.8 to 9.1 m)	−35° to −20°F (−37° to −29°C)	Small spikes of white flowers
Lonicera fragrantissima (winter honeysuckle)	D/E	3 to 15 ft (.9 to 4.5 m)	−10° to −5°F (−23° to −20°C)	Early, fragrant flowers
L. maackii (Amur honeysuckle)	D	15 ft (4.5 m)	−50° to −35°F (−45° to −37°C)	Holds leaves late into fall
L. tatarica (Tatarian honeysuckle)	D	10 ft (3 m)	−35° to −20°F (−37° to −29°C)	Small pink flowers in late spring
Mahonia aquifolium (Oregon grape)	SE/E	3 to 5 ft (.9 to 1.5 m)	−10° to −5°F (−23° to −20°C)	Handsome foliage
M. repens (creeping mahonia)	SE/E	1 ft (.3 m)	−10° to −5°F (−23° to −20°C)	Small; good ground cover
Nandina domestica (heavenly bamboo)	SE/E	8 ft (2.4 m)	5° to 10°F (−15° to −12°C)	Red berries in winter
Nerium oleander (common oleander)	E	15 ft (4.5 m)	5° to 20°F (−15° to −7°C)	Flowering shrub; poisonous juice
Osmanthus heterophyllus (holly olive)	E	18 ft (5.5 m)	−5° to 5°F (−20° to −15°C)	Sun or shade
Phormium tenax (New Zealand flax)	E	15 ft (4.5 m)	10° to 20°F (−12° to −7°C)	Many hybrids
Photinia serrulata (Chinese photinia)	E	30 to 40 ft (9.1 to 12.2 m)	5° to 10°F (−15° to −12°C)	Bright red berries
Pieris floribunda (mountain andromeda)	E	5 ft (1.5 m)	−20° to −10°F (−29° to −23°C)	Does well in dry soil

Botanical and Common Name	Type	Approx. Height	Minimum Night Temp.	Remarks
P. japonica (Japanese andromeda)	E	9 ft (2.7 m)	−10° to −5°F (−23° to −20°C)	Splendid color
Pittosporum tobira (Japanese pittosporum)	E	10 ft (3 m)	10° to 20°F (−12° to −7°C)	Fragrant white flowers
Poncirus trifoliata (hardy orange)	D	30 ft (9.1 m)	−5° to 5°F (−20° to −15°C)	Dense growth; attractive foliage
Potentilla fruitcosa (shrubby cinquefoil)	D	2 to 5 ft (.6 to 1.5 m)	−50° to −35°F (−45 to −37°C)	Many varieties
Prunus laurocerasus (cherry laurel)	E	5 ft (1.5 m)	10° to 20°F (−12° to −7°C)	Many varieties
Pyracantha coccinea (scarlet fire thorn)	E	8 to 10 ft (2.4 to 3 m)	−5° to 5°F (−20° to −15°C)	Many varieties
Raphiolepis umbellata (hawthorn)	E	6 ft (1.8 m)	5° to 10°F (−15° to −12°C)	Sun or partial shade
Ribes sanguineum (flowering currant)	D	4 to 12 ft (1.2 to 3.7 m)	−10° to −5°F (−23° to −20°C)	Deep red flowers March to June
Salix caprea (French pussy willow)	D	25 ft (7.6 m)	−20° to −10°F (−29° to −23°C)	Vigorous grower
S. repens (creeping willow)	D	3 ft (.9 m)	−20° to −10°F (−20° to −23°C)	Good low willow for poor soil
Sarococca ruscifolia (fragrant sweet box)	E	6 ft (1.8 m)	5° to 10°F (−15° to −12°C)	Takes shade
Skimmia japonica (Japanese skimmia)	E	4 ft (1.2 m)	5° to 10°F (−15° to −12°C)	For shade
Spiraea arguta (spiraea)	D	6 ft (1.8 m)	−20° to −10°F (−29° to −23°C)	Free-flowering
S. prunifolia (bridal wreath spiraea)	D	9 ft (2.7 m)	−20° to −10°F (−29° to −23°C)	Turns orange in fall
S. thunbergii (Thunberg spiraea)	D	5 ft (1.5 m)	−20° to −10°F (−29° to −23°C)	Arching branches
S. veitchii (Chinese spiraea)	D	12 ft (3.7 m)	−10° to −5°F (−23° to −20°C)	Good as background
Syringa henryi 'Lutece' (early lilac)	D	10 ft (3 m)	−50° to −35°F (−45° to −37°C)	Early June bloom
S. villosa (late lilac)	D	9 ft (2.7 m)	−50° to −35°F (−45° to −37°C)	Dense, upright habit

Botanical and Common Name	Type	Approx. Height	Minimum Night Temp.	Remarks
S. vulgaris (common lilac)	D	20 ft (6 m)	−35° to −20°F (−37° to −29°C)	Many varieties
Tamarix aphylla (Athel tree)	E	30 to 50 ft (9.1 to 15.2 m)	5° to 10°F (−15° to −12°C)	Good wide-spread tree
T. parviflora 'Pink Cascade', 'Summer Glow' (Albanian tamarick)	D	15 ft (4.5 m)	−20° to −10°F (−29° to −23°C)	Prune right after bloom
Taxus canadensis (Canada yew)	E	3 to 6 ft (.9 to 1.8 m)	−50° to −35°F (−45° to −37°C)	Will tolerate shade
Viburnum davidii (Chinese viburnum)	D	3 ft (.9 m)	5° to 10°F (−15° to −12°C)	Handsome leaves
V. dentatum (arrowwood)	D	15 ft (4.5 m)	−50° to −35°F (−45° to −37°C)	Red fall color
V. dilatatum (linden viburnum)	D	9 ft (2.7 m)	−10° to −5°F (−23° to −20°C)	Colorful red fruit
V. lantana (wayfaring tree)	D	15 ft (4.5 m)	−35° to −20°F (−37° to −29°C)	Grows in dry soil
V. lentago (nannyberry)	D	30 ft (9.1 m)	−50° to −35°F (−45° to −37°C)	Good background or screen plant
V. opulus (European cranberry bush)	D	12 ft (3.7 m)	−35° to −20°F (−37° to −29°C)	Many varieties
V. prunifolium (black haw)	D	15 ft (4.5 m)	−35° to −20°F (−37° to −29°C)	Good specimen plant
V. sieboldii (siebold viburnum)	D	30 ft (4.1 m)	−20° to −10°F (−29° to −23°C)	Stellar performer
V. trilobum (cranberry bush)	D	12 ft (3.7 m)	−50° to −35°F (−45° to −37°C)	Effective in winter
Vitex agnus-castus (chaste tree)	D	9 ft (2.7 m)	−5° to 10°F (−20° to −12°C)	Lilac flowers
Weigela 'Bristol Ruby'	D	7 ft (2.1 m)	−10° to −5°F (−23° to −20°C)	Complex hybrid
W. 'Bristol Snowflake'	D	7 ft (2.1 m)	−10° to −5°F (−23° to −20°C)	Complex hybrid
W. florida (Korean weigela)	D	9 ft (2.1 m)	−10° to −5°F (−23° to −20°C)	Many available
W. middenforfiana (Japanese weigala)	D	1 ft (.3 m)	−20° to −10°F (−29° to −23°C)	Dense, broad shrubs

Type: SE semi-evergreen; D deciduous; E evergreen

Trees for the Small Property

Botanical and Common Name	Type	Approx. Height	Minimum Night Temp.	Remarks
Abies balsamea (balsam fir)	E	70 ft (21.3 m)	−35° to −20°F (−37° to −29°C)	Handsome ornamental
A. concolor (white fir)	E	100 ft (30.4 m)	−20° to −10°F (−29° to −23°C)	Good land-scape tree
Acacia baileyana (Bailey acacia)	E	20 to 30 ft (6 to 9.1 m)	30° to 40°F (−1° to 4°C)	Profuse yellow flowers
Acer circinatum (vine maple)	D	25 ft (7.6 m)	−10° to −5°F (−23° to −20°C)	Small, compact size
A. ginnala (Amur maple)	D	20 ft (6 m)	−50° to −35°F (−45° to −37°C)	Red fall color
A. palmatum (Japanese maple)	D	20 ft (6 m)	−10° to 0°F (−23° to −18°C)	Needs rich, well-drained soil
A. platanoides (Norway maple)	D	90 ft (27.4 m)	−35° to −20°F (−37° to −29°C)	Grows rapidly
A. rubrum (red maple)	D	120 ft (36.6 m)	−35° to −20°F (−37° to −29°C)	Best show in late spring
A. saccharum (sugar maple)	D	120 ft (36.6 m)	−35° to −20°F (−37° to −29°C)	Several varieties
A. spicatum (mountain maple)	D	25 ft (7.6 m)	−50° to −35°F (−45° to −37°C)	Grows in shade
A. tataricum (Tatarian maple)	D	30 ft (9.1 m)	−20° to −10°F (−29° to −23°C)	Good small tree
Aesculus carnea (red horse chestnut)	D	60 ft (18.3 m)	−35° to −20°F (−37° to −29°C)	No autumn color
A. glabra (Ohio buckeye)	D	30 ft (9.1 m)	−35° to −20°F (−37° to −29°C)	Good autumn color
Ailanthus altissima (tree-of-heaven)	D	60 ft (18.3 m)	−20° to −10°F (−29° to −23°C)	Very adaptable
Albizia julibrissin (silk tree)	D	20 ft (6 m)	5° to 10°F (−15° to −12°C)	Very ornamental
Alnus glutinosa (black alder)	D	70 ft (21.3 m)	−35° to −20°F (−37° to −29°C)	Tolerates wet soil
A. incana (common alder)	D	60 ft (18.3 m)	−50° to −35°F (−45° to −37°C)	Round-headed habit

Botanical and Common Name	Type	Approx. Height	Minimum Night Temp.	Remarks
Bauhinia blakeana (orchid tree)	E	20 ft (6 m)	30° to 40°F (–1° to 4°C)	Abundant flowers; partially deciduous
Betula papyrifera (canoe birch)	D	90 ft (27.4 m)	–50° to –35°F (–45° to –37°C)	Stellar ornamental
B. pendula (European birch)	D	60 ft (18.3 m)	–40° to –30°F (–40° to –34°C)	Graceful, but short-lived
B. populifolia (gray birch)	D	40 ft (12.2 m)	–20° to –10°F (–29° to –23°C)	Yellow color in autumn
Carya glabra (pignut)	D	120 ft (36.6 m)	–20° to –10°F (–29° to –23°C)	Slow grower
C. ovata (shagbark hickory)	D	130 ft (39.6 m)	–30° to –10°F (–34° to –23°C)	Narrow, upright habit
Castanea mollissima (Chinese chestnut)	D	60 ft (18.3 m)	–20° to –10°F (–29° to –23°C)	Round-headed, dense tree
Catalpa speciosa (western catalpa)	D	50 ft (15.2 m)	–20° to –10°F (–29° to –23°C)	Large white flowers
Cedrus atlantica (atlas cedar)	E	100 ft (30.4 m)	–5° to 5°F (–20° to –15°C)	Nice pyramid
Celtis occidentalis (hackberry)	D	75 ft (22.9 m)	–50° to –35°F (–45° to –37°C)	Good shade tree
Cercis canadensis (eastern redbud)	D	25 ft (7.6 m)	–20° to –10°F (–29° to –23°C)	Lovely flowers
Chamaecyparis obtusa (Hinoki false cypress)	E	130 ft (39.6 m)	–20° to –10°F (–29° to –23°C)	Broadly pyramidal
C. pisifera (sawara false cypress)	D	100 ft (30.4 m)	–35° to –20°F (–37° to –29°C)	Many varieties
Chionanthus virginicus (fringe tree)	D	20 ft (6 m)	–20° to –10°F (–29° to –23°C)	Bountiful flowers
Cinnamomum camphora (camphor tree)	E	40 ft (12.2 m)	20° to 30°F (–7° to –1°C)	Dense branching habit
Cornus florida (flowering dogwood)	D	25 ft (7.6 m)	–30° to –10°F (–34° to –23°C)	Stellar ornamental
C. kousa (Japanese dogwood)	D	20 ft (6 m)	–10° to –5°F (–23° to –20°C)	Lovely flowers in June

Botanical and Common Name	Type	Approx. Height	Minimum Night Temp.	Remarks
Cotinus americanus (American smoke tree)	D	25 ft (7.6 m)	−10° to −5°F (−23° to −20°C)	Outstanding fall color
Crataegus mollis (downy hawthorn)	D	30 ft (9.1 m)	−20° to −10°F (−29° to −23°C)	Pear-shaped red fruit
C. oxyacantha (English hawthorn)	D	20 ft (6 m)	−20° to −10°F (−29° to −23°C)	Pink to red flowers
C. phaenopyrum (Washington hawthorn)	D	30 ft (9.1 m)	−20° to −10°F (−29° to −23°C)	Profuse flowers, brilliant autumn color
Cryptomeria japonica 'Lobbi' (Japanese cedar)	E	30 to 50 ft (9.1 to 15.2 m)	−5° to 5°F (−20° to −15°C)	Pyramidal shape
Diospyros virginiana (common persimmon)	D	40 ft (12.2 m)	−10° to −5°F (−23° to −20°C)	Round-headed habit
Elaeagnus angustifolia (Russian olive)	D	20 ft (6 m)	−50° to −35°F (−45° to −37°C)	Vigorous; any soil
Eriobotrya japonica (loquat)	E	20 ft (6 m)	5° to 10°F (−15° to −12°C)	Needs well-drained soil
Eucalyptus camaldulensis (red gum)	E	80 to 100 ft (24.4 to 30.4 m)	20° to 30°F (−7° to −1°C)	Fine landscape tree
E. globulus (blue gum)	E	200 ft (61 m)	20° to 30°F (−7° to −1°C)	Good windbreak
E. gunnii (cider gum)	E	40 to 75 ft (12.2 to 22.9 m)	0° to 10°F (−18° to −12°C)	Shade or screen tree
E. polyanthemos (silver-dollar gum)	E	20 to 60 ft (6 to 18.3 m)	10° to 20°F (−12° to −7°C)	Fine landscape tree
Fagus grandifolia (American beech)	D	120 ft (36.6 m)	−35° to −20°F (−37° to −29°C)	Stellar tree
F. sylvatica (European beech)	D	100 ft (30.4 m)	−20° to −10°F (−29° to −23°C)	Several varieties
Franklinia alatamaha (Franklin tree)	D	30 ft (9.1 m)	−10° to 0°F (−23° to −18°C)	Large white-red foliage in autumn
Fraxinus americana (white ash)	D	120 ft (36.6 m)	−35° to −20°F (−37° to −29°C)	Grows in almost any soil
F. holotricha (Balkan ash)	D	35 ft (10.6 m)	−10° to −5°F (−23° to −20°C)	Fast, low-growing shade tree

Botanical and Common Name	Type	Approx. Height	Minimum Night Temp.	Remarks
F. ornus (flowering ash)	D	35 ft (10.6 m)	−10° to 0°F (−23° to −18°C)	Dense foliage; pretty flowers
Ginkgo biloba (maidenhair tree)	D	120 ft (36.6 m)	−20° to −10°F (−29° to −23°C)	Popular
Gleditsia aquatica (water locust)	D	60 ft (18.3 m)	−5° to 5°F (−20° to −15°C)	Needs moist place
G. triacanthos (sweet honey locust)	D	100 ft (30.4 m)	−20° to −10°F (−29° to −23°C)	Several varieties
Jacaranda acutifolia (green ebony)	D	50 ft (15.2 m)	30° to 40°F (−1° to 4°C)	Blue flowers in summer
Juniperus virginiana (eastern red cedar)	E	30 to 50 ft (9.1 to 15.2 m)	−50° to −35°F (−45° to −37°C)	Slow growing
Koelreuteria paniculata (golden-rain tree)	D	30 ft (9.1 m)	−10° to −5°F (−23° to −20°C)	Magnificent summer bloom
Laburnum watereri (golden-chain tree)	D	25 ft (7.6 m)	−10° to −5°F (−23° to −20°C)	Deep yellow flowers
Liquidambar styraciflua (sweet gum)	D	90 ft (27.4 m)	−10° to −5°F (−23° to −20°C)	Beautiful symmetry
Liriodendron tulipfera (tulip tree)	D	100 ft (30.4 m)	−20° to −10°F (−29° to −23°C)	Robust grower
Magnolia soulangiana (saucer magnolia)	D	25 ft (7.6 m)	−10° to −5°F (−23° to −20°C)	Many types; also ever- greens and shrubs
M. stellata (star magnolia)	D	20 ft (6 m)	−10° to −5°F (−23° to −20°C)	Very ornamental
Malus baccata (Siberian crab apple)	D	45 ft (13.7 m)	−50° to −35°F (−45° to −37°C)	Lovely flowers and fruit
M. floribunda (Japanese flowering crab apple)	D	30 ft (9.1 m)	−20° to −10°F (−29° to −23°C)	Handsome foliage and flowers
Phellodendron amurense (cork tree)	D	50 ft (15.2 m)	−35° to −20°F (−37° to−29°C)	Massive branches; wide open habit
Picea abies 'Excelsa' (Norway spruce)	E	75 ft (22.9 m)	−50° to −35°F (−45° to−37°C)	Not for small grounds

Botanical and Common Name	Type	Approx. Height	Minimum Night Temp.	Remarks
Pinus bungeana (lace-bark pine)	E	75 ft (22.9 m)	−20° to −10°F (−29° to −23°C)	Slow-growing tree
P. densiflora (Japanese red pine)	E	80 ft (24.4 m)	−20° to −10°F (−29° to−23°C)	Flat-top habit
P. nigra (Austrian pine)	E	90 ft (27.4 m)	−20° to −10°F (−29° to −23°C)	Fast-growing tree
P. parviflora (Japanese white pine)	E	90 ft (27.4 m)	−10° to −5°F (−23° to −20°C)	Handsome ornamental
P. ponderosa (ponderosa pine)	E	150 ft (45.7 m)	−10° to −5°F (−23° to −20°C)	Rapid growth
P. thunbergiana (Japanese black pine)	E	90 ft (27.4 m)	−20° to −10°F (−29° to −23°C)	Dense, spreading tree
Platanus acerifolia (plane tree)	D	100 ft (30.4 m)	−10° to −5°F (−23° to −20°C)	Popular street tree
P. occidentalis (buttonwood)	D	100+ ft (30.4+ m)	−20° to −10°F (−29° to −23°C)	Heavy frame
Podocarpus gracilior (fern pine)	E	60 ft (18.3 m)	30° to 40°F (−1° to 4°C)	Robust grower
P. macrophyllus (yew pine)	E	60 ft (18.3m)	5° to 10°F (−15° to −12°C)	Grows untended
Populus alba (white poplar)	D	90 ft (27.4 m)	−35° to −20°F (−37° to −29°C)	Wide-spreading tree
P. canadensis 'Eugenei' (Carolina poplar)	D	100 ft (30.4 m)	−20° to −10°F (−29° to −23°C)	Vagrant roots
Prunus amygdalus (almond)	D	25 ft (7.6 m)	−5° to 5°F (−20° to −15°C)	Handsome pink flowers
P. serotina (black cherry)	D	100 ft (30.4 m)	−20° to −10°F (−29° to −23°C)	Handsome foliage; many varieties; some evergreen
P. serrulata (Japanese flowering cherry)	D	25 ft (7.6 m)	−10° to 0°F (−23° to −18°C)	Low grower; many kinds; some evergreen
P. triloba (flowering almond)	D	10 ft (3 m)	−10° to −5°F (−23° to −20°C)	One of the best; sometimes classed as a shrub

Botanical and Common Name	Type	Approx. Height	Minimum Night Temp.	Remarks
Quercus alba (white oak)	D	80 ft (24.4 m)	−20° to −10°F (−29° to −23°C)	Needs room to grow
Q. coccinea (scarlet oak)	D	80 ft (24.4 m)	−20° to −10°F (−29° to −23°C)	Brilliant autumn color
Q. palustris (pin oak)	D	120 ft (36.6 m)	−20° to −10°F (−29° to −23°C)	Beautiful pyramid
Q. rubra (red oak)	D	80 ft (24.4 m)	−35° to −20°F (−37° to −29°C)	Oval round top tree
Robinia pseudoacacia (black locust)	D	80 ft (24.4 m)	−35° to −20°F (−37° to −29°C)	Fine, late spring flowers
Salix alba (white willow)	D	40 ft (12.2 m)	−50° to −35°F (−45° to −37°C)	Good upright willow
S. babylonica (weeping willow)	D	40 ft (12.2 m)	−10° to −5°F (−23° to −20°C)	Fast grower
Sophora japonica (Japanese pagoda tree)	D	60 ft (18.3 m)	−20° to −10°F (−29° to −23°C)	Good shade tree
Sorbus aucuparia (mountain ash)	D	45 ft (13.7 m)	−35° to −20°F (−37° to −29°C)	Red autumn color
Taxus baccata (English yew)	E	60 ft (18.3 m)	−5° to 5°F (−20° to −15°C)	Best among yews
T. cuspidata 'Capitata' (Japanese yew)	E	50 ft (15.2 m)	−20° to −10°F (−29° to −23°C)	Good landscape tree
Thuja occidentalis (American arborvitae)	E	65 ft (19.8 m)	−50° to −35°F (−45° to −37°C)	Sometimes needles turn brown in winter
Tilia americana (American linden)	D	90 ft (27.4 m)	−50° to −35°F (−45° to −37°C)	Fragrant white flowers in July
T. cordata (small-leaved linden)	D	60 ft (18.3 m)	−35° to −20°F (−37° to −29°C)	Dense habit
T. tomentosa (silver linden)	D	80 ft (24.4 m)	−20° to −10°F (−29° to −23°C)	Beautiful specimen tree
Tsuga canadendis (Canada hemlock)	E	75 ft (22.9 m)	−35° to −20°F (−37° to −29°C)	Many uses; hedges, screens and landscaping
T. caroliniana (Carolina hemlock)	E	75 ft (22.9 m)	−20° to −10°F (−29° to −23°C)	Fine all-purpose evergreen

Botanical and Common Name	Type	Approx. Height	Minimum Night Temp.	Remarks
T. diversifolia (Japanese hemlock)	E	90 ft (27.4 m)	–10° to –5°F (–23° to –20°C)	Good evergreen
Ulmus americana (American elm)	D	100 ft (30.4 m)	–50° to –35°F (–45° to –37°C)	Most popular shade tree
Umbellularia californica (California laurel)	E	75 ft (22.9 m)	5° to 10°F (–15° to –12°C)	Favorite West Coast tree

Type: E Evergreen, D Deciduous

VINES

In the small garden, vines and trailers serve a dual purpose: they are decorative, and they can become a leafy green wall for privacy or shade. Properly selected for texture and size, they can make a small area seem larger and also cover an unsightly wall or fence.

With contemporary architecture, which often uses bare expanses of walls and sometimes rather sterile lines, vines become an essential part of any good landscape plan. They are stellar decoration for screening walls or fences or blocking out an objectionable view. They fit into small spaces and can assume many shapes—the flowering kinds are breathtaking in bloom.

There are numerous vines to use, some more effective in one area than another. Several offer fine flowers; others are valued for their rich texture or exquisite leaf patterns. Vines can become a highly ornamental part of the small garden, but they must be pruned and trained to a desired shape to create handsome compositions.

Some of the climbing vines, like clematis, bougainvillea and morning-glory, can become delightful screens of living color with proper care. Vines such as stephanotis, wisteria, and sweet pea have a dainty loveliness about them and a fragile quality that is often necessary to soften harsh garden walls and house lines. And many vines—euonymus, bittersweet, pyracantha—have colorful winter berries that are indispensable in the snow landscape.

SUITABLE SUPPORTS

Many vines climb by means of twining stems that need support; others have tendrils or discs. Some vines have leaflike appendages that act as tendrils, grasping the object on which they grow. Other plants, like jasmine, have long, slender, arching stems and need support: some, such as ivy geranium and trailing lantana, are prostrate in growth. Along with growth habit, vines may be either delicate or heavy with masses of foliage. Several varieties grow rapidly in a few months; others take years to fill a space. Select vines carefully; do not choose them indiscriminately or constant care may be needed.

Few vines will look good or thrive without a support—a trellis, wood grid or a wall; they become vagrant and lose their vine characteristics. If there is no wall, a support must be furnished that is sturdy enough to hold the weight of the vine. Metal frame lattices are good, and so are heavy duty wooden ones. You will find special nails and other attaching devices for vines at nurseries. Some vines, like ficus or ivy, are clingers and only need a stone or brick wall for support. Others, like wisteria, climb by stems and need a lattice or fence-type support.

VINES AS GARDEN PLANTS

Many vines are annuals or are treated as annuals in the northern part of the United States. They are showy for a long time in summer and can be started in tubs, if desired, in early spring. In northern locations start the plants indoors in a warm, sunny place about eight weeks before the last frost-free days by putting seeds into 5-inch (12.7-cm) diameter pots. When warm weather starts, place the pots outside. A perennial vine is a plant that lasts for many years, old roots sprouting new growth each spring. They are easily grown once established, but like all vines they will need periodic pruning and shaping.

Some plants can grow untended; vines cannot. Water and good soil are necessary requirements, of course, but most vines will tolerate some neglect in this arena. However, these green traceries must be kept in bounds by pruning and by intelligent shaping. A vine that is not meticulously trained becomes an eyesore—especially in a small garden. Do not let the plant get so lush that it gets tangled in its own growth.

For vines growing on a flat surface like a wall or fence, selection of suitable varieties with handsome leaves is essential. Pay attention to leaf size and texture; fine, small leaves cloak a wall handsomely and, to some extent, larger-leaved species can be used too. For vines trained overhead or on a trellis, leaf pattern is not as important; flowers are perhaps more desirable here, for a living ceiling of color is dramatic indeed and can make the small garden a veritable wonderland.

Plant woody vines in a deep planting hole to a depth of about 3 to 4 feet (.9 to 1.2 m) so that the roots will have ample growing space. Replace the dug-out soil with good topsoil, but do not include manure or fertilizers that may burn the plants. When the plant is in place, tamp the earth gently around the collar of the plant so that air pockets will not form. Water thoroughly and deeply, and for the first few weeks give the plant some extra attention. (This merely means watching it to see that it is getting started.) Once established, it can have routine care.

Choose vines carefully, provide suitable supports and keep them well trained; you will be amazed at what they can do for the garden. However, they are essentially outlaws and will, if not stopped, grow over their neighboring plants. Remember too that once in place against a wall, a vine is difficult to remove in order to paint that wall, so choose plants accordingly.

Vines for the Small Property

Botanical and Common Name	Minimum Night Temperature	General Description	Sun or Shade	Remarks
Akebia quinata (fiveleaf akebia)	−20° to −10°F (−29° to −23°C)	Vigorous twiner with fragrant small flowers	Sun or partial shade	Needs support; prune in fall or early spring
Allamanda cathartica (golden trumpet)	Tender	Dense with heavy stems and lovely tubular flowers	Sun	Prune in early spring
Ampelopsis brevipedunculata (porcelain ampelopsis, blueberry climber)	−20° to −10°F (−29° to −23°C)	Strong grower with dense leaves	Sun or shade	Prune in early spring
Antigonon leptosus (coral vine, queen's-wreath)	Tender	Excellent as screen	Sun	Needs light support; prune after bloom
Aristolochia durior (Dutchman's-pipe)	−20° to −10°F (−29° to −23°C)	Big twiner with mammoth leaves	Sun or shade	Needs sturdy support; prune in spring or summer

Botanical and Common Name	Minimum Night Temperature	General Description	Sun or Shade	Remarks
Celastrus scandens (American bittersweet)	–50° to –35°F (–45° to –37°C)	Light green leaves with red berries	Sun or shade	Prune in early spring before growth starts
Clematis armandii (evergreen clematis)	5° to 10°F (–15° to –23°C)	Lovely flowers and foliage; many colors	Sun	Needs support; prune lightly after bloom
Clytostoma (*Bignonia capreolata*, cross vine, trumpet vine)	–5° to 5°F (–20° to –15°C)	Orange flowers	Sun or shade	Thin out weak branches in spring; clings by discs
Doxantha unguis-cati (cat's claw)	10° to 20° F (–12° to –7°C)	Dark green leaves with yellow blooms	Sun	Needs no support; prune after bloom
Euonymus fortunei (winter creeper)	–35° to –20°F (–37° to –29°)	Shiny leathery leaves; orange berries in fall	Sun or shade	Needs support; prune in early spring
Fatshedera lizei (ivy tree)	20° to 30°F (–7° to –1°C)	Grown for handsome foliage	Shade	No pruning needed
Ficus pumila (creeping fig)	20° to 30°F (–7° to –1°C)	Small heart-shaped leaves	Partial shade	Thin plant in late fall or early spring
Gelsemium sempervirens (Carolina jessamine)	Tender	Fragrant yellow flowers	Sun or partial shade	Needs support; thin plant immediately after bloom
Hedera helix (English ivy)	–10° to – 5°F (–23° to –20°C)	Scalloped, neat leaves; many varieties	Shade	Prune and thin in early spring
Hydrangea petiolaris (climbing hydrangea)	–20° to –10°F (–29° to –23°C)	Scalloped, neat flowers	Shade or partial shade	Thin and prune in winter or early spring
Ipomoea purpurea (morning-glory)	Tender	White, blue, purple, pink or red flowers	Sun	Blooms until frost
Jasminum nudiflorum (winter jasmine)	–10° to –5°F (–23° to –20°C)	Yellow flowers	Sun or shade	Needs strong support; thin and shape annually after bloom
J. officinale (white jasmine)	5° to 10°F (–15° to –12°C)	Showy, dark green leaves with white flowers	Sun or shade	Provide strong support; thin and shape after bloom
Kadsura japonica (scarlet kadsura)	5° to 10°F (–15° to –12°C)	Bright red berries in fall	Sun	Provide support; prune annually in early spring

Botanical and Common Name	Minimum Night Temperature	General Description	Sun or Shade	Remarks
Lonicera caprifolium (sweet honeysuckle)	−10° to −5°F (−23° to −20°C)	White or yellow trumpet flowers	Sun	Prune in fall or spring
L. hildebrandiana (Burmese fall honeysuckle)	20° to 30°F (−7° to −1°C)	Shiny, dark green leaves	Sun or partial shade	Needs support; prune in late fall
L. japonica 'Halliana' (Hall's honeysuckle, Japanese honeysuckle)	−20° to −10°F (−29° to −23°C)	Deep green leaves; bronze in fall	Sun or shade	Provide support; prune annually in fall and spring
Mandevilla suaveolens (Chilean jasmine)	20° to 30°F (−7° to −1°C)	Heart-shaped leaves and flowers	Sun	Trim and cut back lightly in fall; remove seed pods as they form
Parthenocissus quinquefolia (Virginia creeper, American ivy)	−35° to −20°F (−37° to −29°C)	Scarlet leaves in fall	Sun or shade	Prune in early spring
Passiflora caerulea (passionflower)	5° to 10°F (−15° to −12°C)	Spectacular flowers	Sun	Needs support; prune hard annually in fall or early spring
Phaseolus coccineus (scarlet runner)	Tender	Bright red flowers	Sun	Renew each spring
Plumbago capensis (plumbago)	20° to 30°F (−7° to −1°C)	Blue flowers	Sun	Prune somewhat in spring
Rosa (rambler rose)	−10° to −5°F (−23° to −20°C)	Many varieties	Sun	Needs support; prune out dead wood, shorten long shoots and cut laterals back to two nodes in spring or early summer after bloom
Smilax rotundifolia (horse brier)	−20° to −10°F (−29° to −23°C)	Glossy green foliage	Sun or shade	Needs no support; prune hard annually any time
Trachelospermum jasminoides (star jasmine)	20° to 30°F (−7° to −1°C)	Dark green leaves with small white flowers	Partial shade	Provide heavy support; prune very lightly in fall
Vitis coignetiae (glory grape)	−10° to 5°F (−23° to −15°C)	Colorful autumn leaves	Sun or partial shade	Provide support; prune annually in fall or spring

Botanical and Common Name	Minimum Night Temperature	General Description	Sun or Shade	Remarks
Wisteria floribunda (Japanese wisteria)	–20° to –10°F (–29° to –23°C)	Violet blue flowers	Sun	Provide support; prune annually once mature to shorten long branches after bloom or in winter; pinch back branches first year

SPECIALTY VINES

TWINING VINES

Akebia quinata (fiveleaf akebia)
Aristolochia durior (Dutchman's-pipe)
Celastrus spp. (bittersweet)
Mandevilla suaveolens (Chilean jasmine)
Smilax rotundifolia (horse brier)
Trachelospermum jasminoides (star jasmine)

CLIMBING VINES

Ampelopsis spp.
Clytostoma, Bignonia capreolata (cross vine, trumpet vine)
Clematis spp.
Doxantha unguis-cati (cat's-claw)
Parthenocissus quinquefolia (Virginia creeper, American ivy)
Passiflora spp. (passion-flower)
Vitis coignetiae (glory grape)

RAPID-GROWING VINES

Akebia quinata (fiveleaf akebia)
Ampelopsis aconitifolia (yellow ampelopsis)
Aristolochia durior (Dutchman's-pipe)
Clematis spp.
Clytosoma, Bignonia capreolata (cross vine, trumpet vine)

Doxantha unguis-cati (cat's-claw)
Ficus pumila (creeping fig)
Hedera helix (English ivy)
Lonicera spp. (honeysuckle)
Trachelospermum jasminoides (star jasmine)
Vitis coignetiae (glory grape)
Wisteria floribunda (Japanese wisteria)
W. sinensis (Chinese wisteria)

VINES FOR FLOWERS

Clytosoma, Bignonia capreolata (cross vine, trumpet vine)
Clematis spp.
Hydrangea petiolaris (climbing hydrangea)
Mandevilla suaveolens (Chilean jasmine)
Passiflora spp. (passion-flower)
Plumbago capensis (plum-bago)
Rosa (rambler rose)
Trachelospermum jasminoides (star jasmine)
Wisteria floribunda (Japanese wisteria)

VINES FOR COLORFUL FRUIT

Celastrus scandens (American bittersweet)
Euonymus fortunei (winter creeper)
Kadsura japonica (scarlet kadsura)
Smilax rotundifolia (horse brier)

❦
The
Flower Garden

Garden flowers are an essential part of the outdoor scene, but too often they *are* the garden. Remember that no matter how beautiful flowers may appear in catalogs and pictures, herbaceous plants—perennials, annuals and biennials—are only part of the picture. Do not stress them too much or your garden will become more of a chore than a charm.

Herbaceous plants die down to the ground after their flowering time, and they do not form a permanent woody growth. They are in no way a structural design element. Plan your garden first the way you want it without flowers; then add the perennials and annuals. Use flowers only for what they are—seasonal color.

THE PLANTING PLAN

Use herbaceous plants for flowering seasons only, and, as mentioned, remember that they do not make a year-round garden. First, plant without them; put in the structure of shrubs and trees so that flowers grown for seasonal accent will be suitably framed all year and will not be missed when they are out of bloom.

For maximum effect, set flowers in curves and frame them with shrub groups, for flowers need a good background to be really effective. With a plain background of sky or fence you will see nothing but empty spaces. Masses of shrubs will show off the blooms and still provide an attractive background. Plant flowers in sweeping arcs and curves; strive for a mass of concentrated color in one area rather than a mixed planting of many colors.

The spring, summer or fall flower garden placed in one area has been greatly recommended by many gardeners. It is beautiful, but generally it requires too much work for the average homeowner and certainly demands utmost arranging skill to be successful.

Keep your flower garden simple, and don't expect continuous color from spring to fall. If a mass of flowers year-round is your goal, use one area for spring bloom, another for summer, and still another for fall. However, because most properties today are small, this is a difficult gardening method.

If you have only one place for flowers, grow mostly perennials and bulbs interplanted with shrubs. Do not rely too much on annuals with short bloom seasons; select the ones that provide color all summer (petunias or snapdragons, for example). Do not put too many varieties in a small area or crowd too great a color range into it. The effect will be a spotty picture.

Consider the shape of flowers as you plant; some are round-headed, others are spiked. The spike forms are sharp accent points in the garden, so do not use too many of them. Place a mass of them in one area, and balance them with another area of round-headed flowers. Also consider the size of the flower. Do not put tiny blooms next to giants or the scale of the arrangement will be disrupted. Arrange gradual changes from tiny to small to medium to large flowers, or vice versa.

With annuals and perennials, plan a concentrated mass or drift. Flower gardening is more working with color than with flowers. A line of blue along a flower bed is not effective in the landscape, but a concentrated mass of blue is indeed dramatic. You want to create free-form, curving masses of color; with rare exceptions plant in a straight line or row. Be bold and imaginative with herbaceous plants, as straight lines of flowers are not attractive. Even though a colored square or rectangle on a broad green canvas can be handsome in some situations, curved forms are more pleasing because they suggest movement.

Principles of Free-form Flower Patterns

Free-form patterns or drifts can take many shapes, but basically they should follow these principles:

1. Use bold curves in small areas.
2. The height of the planting should have some relation to the width of the bed.
3. Do not plan outcurves at lot corners; you want to create a sense of space there.
4. Use heavy and high plantings in the curve and lighter plantings in the bays.

The flower garden can be almost any shape and width, but remember that you have to get to the flowers at the back without stepping over those in the front. (The width should not exceed 30 inches [76.2 cm].) Put tall flowers at the rear, medium-sized ones in the middle, and the smallest growers up front. Intersperse them with larger clumps of medium-sized varieties in the background and foreground to relieve monotony.

Annuals and biennials are generally raised from seed; perennials are best bought as seedlings at nurseries.

COLOR AND ITS EFFECT

When you are working with flower color, know the elements of value, hue and intensity so that you can use flowers intelligently.

Value is the lightness and darkness of a color. Hue is the gradation or actual color—red or orange separated by the warm colors of yellow, orange, scarlet or crimson, for example. (The cool hues include blue, green, purple and their derivatives.) There are several shades of one color, from pale to dark; this difference in tones is the intensity of a color.

To use color effectively, first decide where there is to be light or dark color, and employ different shades in rhythmic steps to achieve a harmonious effect—say, pale pink, medium pink and dark or intense pink. If you want a dark color to predominate, have dark-colored flowers; to stress a light color, use light-colored flowers.

When you work with warm colors, for example, begin with red, followed by orange-red, orange, pale orange, orange-yellow, pale yellow, beige, ending with white. Follow a very gradual sequence rather than switching from orange to white and creating a jarring effect. A monochromatic color scheme is the most effective way to display flowers in the garden. With cool colors start with blue and finish with purple, again building up gradually rather than abruptly.

CULTURE

With few exceptions, annuals, perennials and biennials will need as much sunlight as they can get. And although soil requirements vary, if drainage is good, most plants will thrive regardless.

For maximum growth provide a neutral soil that is reasonably light in texture and a good amount of humus.

If you want lots of flowers, always keep the flower bed evenly moist. Herbaceous plants can take great quantities of water; the soil should never be dry. The key to a lush and colorful flower garden is to water plants thoroughly and deeply, especially on hot, sunny days. Sometimes in August I sprinkle plants from early morning to noon.

Keep the soil weeded; mulching it will save much work (see Chapter Eleven). Feed annuals and perennials a few weeks after they are planted and then at monthly intervals. Established perennials need feeding as soon as growth starts in the spring and again at four- to six-week intervals until they bloom.

The following is a mere sampling of flowers. We have not included varieties because of space, but all suppliers list special varieties of outstanding color; consult nursery catalogs for their descriptions.

Colorful Perennials and Biennials
For the Small Property

Achillea ptarmica (yarrow or sneezewort)—white flowers in summer or fall; grows to 18 inches (45.7 cm).

Alcea rosea (hollyhock)—most colors except true blue and green; lovely autumn flowers; grows to 10 feet (3 m).

Anchusa capensis (summer forget-me-not)—pure bright blue blooms in early summer; grows to 18 inches (45.7 cm); needs sunlight or light shade.

Anemone japonica (Japanese anemone)—white, pink, or rose flowers in fall; grows to 48 inches (122 cm); needs sunlight or light shade.

Anthemis tinctoria (golden Marguerite)—yellow flowers in summer or fall; grows to 36 inches (91.4 cm).

Arabis caucasica (wall rock cress)—white flowers in early spring; grows to 10 inches (25.4 cm); needs sunlight or light shade.

Artemisia albula (wormwood)—silver-gray blooms in summer and fall; grows to 48 inches (122 cm).

Asclepias tuberosa (butterfly weed)—orange flowers in summer; grows to 36 inches (91.4 cm).

Aster novae-angliae (New England aster)—mainly blue and purple flowers in fall; grows to 5 feet (1.5 m).

Begonia semperflorens (wax begonia)—white, pink and deep rose flowers all summer; grows to 18 inches (45.7 cm); needs sunlight or shade.

Bergenia cordifolia (heartleaf bergenia)—white or rose flowers in early summer; grows to 18 inches (45.7 cm); needs sunlight or light shade.

Campanula persicifolia (willow bellflower)—white or blue flowers in summer; grows to 36 inches (91.4 cm).

Chrysanthemum coccineum (pyrethum or painted daisy)—white, pink or red blooms in early summer; grows to 36 inches (91.4 cm).

C. maximum (Shasta daisy)—white flowers in summer and fall; grows to 48 inches (122 cm).

Coreopsis grandiflora (tick-seed)—golden yellow flowers in summer; grows to 36 inches (91.4 cm).

Delphinium hybrid (Connecticut Yankee)—blue, violet or white flowers in early summer; grows to 36 inches (91.4 cm).

Dianthus barbatus (sweet William)—white, pink, red or rose flowers in early summer; grows to 24 inches (61 cm); needs sunlight or light shade.

Dicentra spectabilis (bleeding-heart)—white, pink or rose flowers in spring; grows to 36 inches (91.4 cm); needs light shade.

Digitalis purpurea (common foxglove)—mixed colors, marked and spotted; blooms in early summer; grows to 30 inches (76.2 cm); needs sunlight or partial shade.

Epimedium grandiflorum (bishop's-hat)—red and violet flowers in summer; grows to 12 inches (30.4 cm); needs light shade.

Felicia amelloides (blue Marguerite)—blue flowers in spring and summer; grows to 24 inches (61 cm).

Gentiana asclepiadea (willow gentian)—blue to violet flowers in late summer; grows to 24 inches (61 cm); needs light shade.

Gypsophila paniculata (baby's-breath)—white flowers all summer; grows to 36 inches (91.4 cm).

Helianthus decapetalus x *multiflorus* (sunflower)—yellow flowers in summer; grows to 48 inches (122 cm).

Hemerocallis spp. (daylily)—all colors but blue, green, violet and true red; blooms in spring and summer; grows to 6 feet (1.8 m); needs sunlight or light shade.

Heuchera sanguinea (coralbells)—red, pink and white flowers in early summer; grows to 18 inches (45.7 cm); needs sunlight or light shade.

Iberis sempervirens (evergreen candytuft)—white flowers in early spring to summer; grows to 12 inches (30.4 cm).

Iris cristata (crested iris)—lavender and light blue flowers in spring; grows to 8 inches (20.3 cm); needs light shade.

I. kaempferi (Japanese iris)—purple, violet, pink, rose, red and white flowers in spring and early summer; grows to 48 inches (122 cm); needs sunlight or light shade.

Lilium spp. (lily)—white, pink, yellow, gold and bicolor flowers in early summer; grows to 7 feet (2.1 m); needs sunlight or light shade.

Linum perenne (blue flax)—sky-blue flowers in summer; grows to 24 inches (61 cm).

Lobelia cardinalis (cardinal flower)—red flowers in late summer; grows to 36 inches (91.4 cm).

Lythrum spp. (loosestrife)—rose to purple flowers in summer; grows to 5 feet (1.5 m); needs sunlight or light shade.

Mertensia virginica (Virginia bluebell or cowslip)—bicolor blue blooms in early spring; grows to 18 inches (45.7 cm); needs light shade.

Monarda didyma (bee balm)—white, pink and scarlet red flowers in summer and fall; grows to 36 inches (91.4 cm).

Papaver orientale (Oriental poppy)—pink, white, scarlet, orange or salmon flowers in early summer; grows to 48 inches (122 cm).

Pentstemon spp. (beard-tongue)—blue, pink and crimson flowers, mostly bicolors, in summer and fall; grows to 36 inches (91.4 cm).

Phlox paniculata (summer perennial phlox)—pink, purple, rose, white, orange and red flowers in late summer to fall; grows to 5 feet (1.5 m).

Physostegia virginiana (false dragonhead)—white and rose bicolors; blooms mid- to late summer; grows to 5 feet (1.5 m).

Polygonatum multiflorum (Solomon's-seal)—white flowers in spring; grows to 12 inches (30.4 cm); needs sunlight or shade.

Primula spp. (primrose)—blooms in bicolors of blue, red and yellow in late spring; grows to 14 inches (35.6 cm).

Rudbeckia hirta (black-eyed Susan)—yellow, pink, orange and white flowers in summer; grows to 48 inches (122 cm).

Scabiosa caucasica (pincushion flower)—white, blue and purple flowers in summer and fall; grows to 30 inches (76.2 cm).

Solidago spp. (goldenrod)—yellow flowers in summer; grows to 24 inches (61 cm); needs sunlight or light shade.

Tritoma (*Kniphofia*; torch lily)—cream, white, yellow and orange flowers in early summer; grows to 6 feet (1.8 m).

Viola cornuta (tufted pansy)—purple flowers, but newer varieties in many colors; blooms in spring and fall; grows to 8 inches (20.3 cm); needs light shade.

Colorful Annuals for the Small Property

Ageratum houstonianum (floss flower)—blue flowers in summer and fall; grows to 22 inches (55.9 cm).

Amaranthus tricolor (Joseph's-coat)—bronze-green crown, foliage marked cream and red; blooms in summer; grows to 7 feet (2.1 m).

Antirrhinum majus (common or large snapdragon)—large choice of colors and flower form; blooms in late spring and fall, and in summer where cool; grows to 48 inches (122 cm).

Begonia semperflorens (wax begonia)—white, pink, and deep rose flowers all summer; grows to 18 inches; needs sunlight or shade.

Calendula officinalis (calendula or pot marigold)—cream, yellow, orange and apricot flowers in winter where mild, late spring elsewhere; grows to 24 inches (61 cm).

Centaurea cyanus (bachelor's-button or cornflower)—blue, pink, wine and white flowers in spring where mild, summer elsewhere; grows to 30 inches (76.2 cm).

Clarkia unguiculata (mountain garland)—white, pink, rose, crimson, purple and salmon blooms; flowers in late spring to early summer; grows to 36 inches (91.4 cm).

Cosmos bipinnatus (cosmos)—white, pink lavender, rose and purple flowers all summer; grows to 6 feet (1.7 m).

Delphinium ajacis (rocket larkspur)—blue, pink, lavender, rose, salmon, carmine and white flowers in late spring to early summer; grows to 5 feet (1.5 m).

Eschscholzia californica (California poppy)—gold, yellow and orange; 'Mission Bell' varieties include pink and rose flowers in winter, and in spring in mild climates; grows to 24 inches (61 cm).

Gomphrena globosa (globe amaranth)—white, crimson, violet, pale gold flowers all summer; heat-resistant; grows to 36 inches (91.4 cm).

Helianthus annuus (common garden sunflower)—yellow and mahogany bicolors or yellow with black centers; blooms in summer; grows to 10 feet (3 m) or more.

Iberis amara (rocket candytuft)—white flowers in late spring; grows to 20 inches (50.8 cm).

Impatiens balsamina (garden balsam)—white, pink, rose and red flowers in summer to fall; grows to 30 inches (76.2 cm); needs light shade, sunlight where cool.

Lathyrus odoratus (winter-flowering sweet pea)—mixed or separate colors, except yellow, orange and green; blooms in late winter where mild; not heat-resistant; grows to 6 feet (1.7 m).

Linum grandiflorum 'Rubrum' (scarlet flax)—scarlet to deep red or rose flowers in late spring and fall; grows to 18 inches (45.7 cm).

Lobularia maritima (sweet alyssum)—white, purple, lavender and rosy pink flowers; blooms year-round where mild, spring to fall elsewhere; grows to 8 inches (20.3 cm).

Matthiola incana (stock)—white, cream, yellow, pink, rose, crimson, red and purple flowers in winters where mild, late spring elsewhere; grows to 36 inches (91.4 cm).

Molucella laevis (shellflower)—green, bell-like bracts resembling flowers; blooms in summer; grows to 30 inches (76.2 cm).

Nemesia strumosa (nemesia)—all colors but green; blooms in spring where mild, early summer elsewhere; grows to 18 inches (45.7 cm).

Nigella damascena (love-in-a-mist)—blue, white and rose-pink flowers in summer; grows to 30 inches (76.2 cm).

Petunia hybrids—all colors except true blue, yellow and orange; blooms summer and fall; grows to 18 inches (45.7 cm).

Physalis alkekengi (Chinese-lantern)—white flowers, orange bracts; blooms in late summer; grows to 24 inches (61 cm); needs sunlight or shade.

Reseda odorata (common mignonette)—greenish brown clusters; blooms in late spring until fall; grows to 18 inches (45.7 cm).

Salpiglossis sinuata (painted-tongue)—flowers have bizarre patterns of red, orange, yellow, pink and purple; blooms in early summer; grows to 36 inches (91.4 cm).

Scabiosa atropurpurea (sweet scabious)—purple, blue, mahogany, white and rose flowers in spring; grows to 36 inches (91.4 cm).

Tagetes erecta (hybrids and species; African or Aztec marigold)— mostly yellow, tangerine and gold flowers; blooms all summer except where hot; grows to 48 inches (122 cm).

T. tenuifolia signata (signet marigold)—small, yellow-orange flowers; blooms all summer except where quite hot; grows to 24 inches (61 cm).

Tropaeolum majus (garden nasturtium)—white, pink, crimson, orange, maroon and yellow flowers in spring and fall, summer where cool; grows to 18 inches (45.7 cm); some spread vigorously; needs sunlight or shade.

Vinca rosea (Madagascar periwinkle)—white and pink flowers, some with contrasting eye; blooms in summer until early fall; grows to 24 inches (61 cm).

Viola tricolor 'Hortensis' (pansy)—"faces" in white, yellow, purple, rose, mahogany, violet and apricot; blooms in spring and fall, winter where mild; grows to 8 inches (20.3 cm).

Garden Flowers for the Small Property

Botanical and Common Name	Approx. Height	Range of Colors	Peak Blooming Season	Light Requirement
Acanthus mollis (Grecian urn)	to 60 in (1.5 m)	White, lilac	Summer	Sun or shade
Achillea ptarmica (yarrow or sneezewort)	to 18 in (45.7 cm)	White	Summer, fall	Sun
Aconitum anthora (monkshood)	36 in (91.4 cm)	Pale yellow	Summer	Sun or shade
Ageratum houstonianum (floss flower)	4 to 22 in (10.2 to 55.9 cm) PD 12 in (30.4 cm)	Blue, pink, white	Summer, fall	Sun or shade
Althaea rosea (hollyhock)	to 10 ft (3 m)	Most colors except true blue and green	Summer	Sun
Alyssum saxatile (basket-of-gold)	8 to 12 in (20.3 to 30.4 cm)	Golden yellow tinged with chartreuse	Early spring	Sun
Amaranthus caudatus (love-lies-bleeding)	3 to 7 ft (.9 to 2.1 m) PD 18 in (45.7 cm)	Red tassel-like flower spikes	Summer	Sun
A. tricolor (Joseph's-coat)	to 4 ft (1.2 m) PD 18 in (45.7 cm)	Bronze-green crown; foliage marked cream and red	Summer	Sun
Anchusa capensis (summer forget-me-not)	12 to 18 in (20.3 to 45.7 cm) PD 6 to 9 in (15.2 to 22.9 cm)	Blue with white throat	Summer	Light shade
Anemone coronaria (poppy-flowered anemone)	to 18 in (45.7 cm)	Red, blue, white	Spring	Sun
A. japonica (Japanese anemone)	2 to 4 ft (.6 to 1.2 m)	White, pink, rose	Fall	Sun or light shade
A. pulsatilla (prairie windflower or pasque flower)	9 to 15 in (22.9 to 38.1 cm)	Lavender to violet	Spring	Sun or light shade
Anthemis tinctoria (golden Marguerite)	2 to 3 ft (.6 to .9 m)	Yellow	Summer, fall	Sun

Botanical and Common Name	Approx. Height	Range of Colors	Peak Blooming Season	Light Requirement
Antirrhinum majus (common or large snapdragon)	1 to 4 ft (.3 to 1.2 m) PD 10 to 18 in (25.4 to 45.7 cm)	Large choice of color	Late spring and fall; summer where cool	Sun
Aquilegia alpina (dwarf columbine)	to 12 in (30.4 cm)	Blue	Early summer	Sun or light shade
Arabis caucasica (wall rock cress)	4 to 10 in (10.2 to 25.4 cm)	White	Early spring	Sun or light shade
Arctotis stoechadi-folia grandis (African daisy)	16 to 24 in (40.6 to 61 cm) PD 10 in (25.4 cm)	Yellow, rust, pink, white	Early spring	Sun
Armeria plataginea (sea pink or thrift)	to 12 in (30.4 cm)	White, dark red, pink	Spring, summer	Sun
Artemisia albula (wormwood)	2 to 4 ft (.6 to 1.2 m)	Silver-gray	Summer, fall	Sun
A. frigida (fringed wormwood or wild sage)	12 to 18 in (30.4 to 45.7 cm)	Silver-white foliage	Summer, fall	Sun
Asclepias tuberosa (butterfly weed)	2 to 3 ft (.6 to .9 m)	Orange	Summer	Sun
Aster frikartii (Frikart aster)	30 to 36 in (76.2 to 91.4 cm)	Blue, lavender	Summer, fall	Sun
A., dwarf type	8 to 15 in (20.3 to 38.1 cm)	Red, blue, purple	Late summer	Sun
A., English hardy (Michaelmas daisy)	30 to 48 in (76.2 to 91.4 cm)	Blue, violet, pink, white	Fall	Sun
Aubrieta deltoidea (common aubrieta or purple rock cress)	2 to 4 in (5 to 10.2 cm)	Blue	Spring	Sun or shade
Begonia semperflorens (wax begonia)	6 to 18 in (15.2 to 45.7 cm) PD 6 to 8 in (15.2 to 20.3 cm)	White, pink, deep-rose; single, double	All summer; perennial in temperate climate	Sun or shade
Bellis perennis (English daisy)	3 to 6 in (7.6 to 15.2 cm)	White, pink, rose	Spring; winter in mild climates	Sun
Bergenia cordifolia (heartleaf bergenia)	12 to 18 in (30.4 to 45.7 cm)	White, rose	Early summer	Sun or light shade

Botanical and Common Name	Approx. Height	Range of Colors	Peak Blooming Season	Light Requirement
Browallia americana (bush violet)	1 to 2 ft (.3 to .6 m) PD 6 to 9 (15.2 to 22.9 cm)	Violet, blue, white	Summer	Sun
Calendula officinalis (calendula or pot marigold)	1 to 2 ft (.3 to .6 m) PD 12 to 15 (30.4 to 38.1 cm)	Cream, yellow, orange, apricot	Winter where mild; late spring elsewhere	Sun
Callistephus chinensis (aster or China aster)	1 to 3 ft (.3 to .9 m) PD 10 in (25.4 cm)	Lavender-blue, white, pink, rose, crimson	Late spring where mild; late summer elsewhere	Sun
Campanula carpatica (bellflower)	8 to 10 in (20.3 to 25.4 cm)	Blue, white	Summer	Sun
C. persicifolia (willow bellflower)	2 to 3 ft (.6 to .9 m)	White, blue	Summer	Sun
Catharanthus roseus (*Vinca rosea* or Madagascar periwinkle)	6 to 24 in (15.2 to 61 cm) PD 12 in (30.4 cm)	White, pink, some with contrasting eye	Summer until early fall	Sun or light shade
Celosia plumosa (plume cockscomb)	1 to 3 ft PD 6 to 12 in (15.2 to 30.4 cm)	Pink, red-gold, yellow	Summer through fall except where hot	Sun or light shade
Centaurea cyanus (bachelor's-button or cornflower)	12 to 30 in (30.4 to 76.2 cm) PD 12 in (30.4 cm)	Blue, pink, wine, white	Spring where mild; summer elsewhere	Sun
C. gymnocarpa (dusty-miller)	18 to 24 in (.6 to .9 m) (45.7 to 61 cm)	Velvety white leaves; purple flowers	Summer	Sun
Chrysanthemum coccineum (pyrethum or painted daisy)	2 to 3 ft (.6 to .9 m)	White, pink, red	Early summer	Sun
C. maximum (Shasta daisy)	2 to 4 ft (.6 to 1.2 m)	White	Summer, fall	Sun or shade
C. morifolium (florist's chrysanthemum)	18 to 30 in (45.7 to 76.2 cm)	Most colors except blue	Late summer, fall	Sun

Botanical and Common Name	Approx. Height	Range of Colors	Peak Blooming Season	Light Requirement
Clarkia amoena (godetia or farewell-to-spring)	18 to 30 in (45.7 to 76.2 cm) PD 9 in (22.9 cm)	Mostly mixed colors; white, pink, salmon, lavender	Late spring; summer where cold	Sun or shade
C. unguiculata (mountain garland)	1 to 3 ft (.3 to .9 m) PD 9 in (22.9 cm)	White, pink, rose, crimson purple, salmon	Late spring to summer	Sun
Cleome spinosa (spider flower)	4 to 5 ft (1.2 to 1.5 m) PD 14 to 16 in (35.6 to 40.6 cm)	Whitish pink	Spring, summer	Sun
Coleus blumei (coleus)	12 to 30 in (30.4 to 76.2 cm) PD 9 to 12 in (22.9 to 30.4 cm)	Grown for its variegated leaves	Midsummer through early fall	Partial shade
Convallaria majalis (lily-of-the-valley)	9 to 12 in (22.9 to 30.4 cm)	White, pink	Spring, early summer	Light to medium shade
Coreopsis grandiflora (tick-seed)	2 to 3 ft (.6 to .9 m)	Golden yellow	Summer	Sun
C. tinctoria (calliopsis)	8 to 30 in (20.3 to 76.2 cm) PD 18 to 24 in (45.7 to 61 cm)	Yellow, orange, maroon, and splashed bicolors	Late spring to summer; late summer where cool	Sun
Cosmos bipinnatus (cosmos)	4 to 6 ft (1.2 to 1.8 m) PD 12 to 15 in (30.4 to 38.1 cm)	White, pink, lavender, rose, purple	All summer	Sun
Delphinium ajacis (rocket larkspur)	to 5 ft (to 1.5 m) PD 9 in (22.9 cm)	Blue, pink, lavender, rose, salmon, carmine, white	Late spring to early summer	Sun
D. hybrid (Connecticut Yankee)	2 to 3 ft (.6 to .9 m)	Blue, violet, white	Early summer	Sun
D. hybrid (Pacific Giant)	4 to 8 ft (1.2 to 2.4 m)	Blue, white	Early summer	Sun
Dianthus barbatus (sweet William)	to 2 ft (.6 m)	White, pink, red	Early summer	Sun or light shade

Botanical and Common Name	Approx. Height	Range of Colors	Peak Blooming Season	Light Requirement
D. deltoides (maiden pink)	8 to 12 in (20.3 to 30.4 cm)	Rose, purple, white	Early summer	Sun
D. spp. (pinks)	6 to 30 in (15.2 to 76.2 cm) PD 4 to 6 in (10.2 to 15.2 cm)	Mostly bicolors of white, pink, lavender, purple	Spring, fall; winter where mild	Sun
Dicentra spectabilis (bleeding-heart)	2 to 3 ft (.6 to .9 m)	Pink, rose, white	Spring	Light shade
Dictamnus albus (gas plant)	3 ft (.9 m)	White, pink, purple	Summer	Sun or light shade
Digitalis purpurea (common foxglove)	18 to 48 in (45.7 to 12.2 cm)	Mixed colors, marked and spotted	Early summer	Partial shade or sun
Dimorphotheca pluvialis (Cape marigold)	4 to 6 in (10.2 to 15.2 cm) PD 12 to 18 in (30.4 to 45.7 cm)	White, yellow, orange, salmon	Winter where mild; summer elsewhere	Sun
Echinops exalatus (globe thistle)	3 to 4 ft (.9 to 1.2 m)	Steel blue	Late summer	Sun
Epimedium grandlflorum (bishop's-hat)	12 in (30.4 cm)	Red, violet	Summer	Light shade
Erysimum asperum (Siberian wall flower)	12 to 18 in (30.4 to 45.7 cm)	Golden orange	Spring	Sun
Eschscholzia californica (California poppy)	1 to 2 ft (.3 to .6 m) PD 9 in (22.9 cm)	Gold, yellow, orange; Mission Bell varieties include pink, rose	Winter; spring in mild climates	Sun
Felicia amelloides (blue Marguerite)	20 to 24 in (50.8 to 6.1 cm)	Blue	Spring, summer	Sun
Gaillardia grandiflora (blanket flower)	2 to 4 ft (.6 to 1.2 m)	Yellow or bicolor	Summer, fall	Sun
G. pulchella (rose-ring gaillardia)	1 to 2 ft (.3 to .6 m) PD 9 in (22.9 cm)	Zoned patterns in warm shades; wine, maroon	All summer	Sun

Botanical and Common Name	Approx. Height	Range of Colors	Peak Blooming Season	Light Requirement
Gazania hybrids (gazania)	10 to 12 in (25.4 to 30.4 cm)	Yellow and brown bicolors	Summer, fall; spring where mild	Sun
Gentiana asclepiadea (willow gentian)	20 to 24 in (50.8 to 61 cm)	Blue to violet	Late summer	Light shade
Geranium grandiflorum (cranesbill)	10 to 12 in (25.4 to 30.4 cm)	Blue marked red	Summer	Light shade
Geum chiloense (*G. coccineum*) (geum)	20 to 24 in (50.8 to 61 cm)	Yellow, red-orange	Early summer	Light shade
Godetia amoena (see *Clarkia amoena*)				
Gomphrena globosa (globe amaranth)	9 to 36 in (22.4 to 91.4 cm) PD 12 in (30.4 cm)	White, crimson, violet, pink	All summer; heat-resistant	Sun
Gypsophila elegans (baby's-breath)	12 to 30 in (30.4 to 76.2 cm) PD 6 in (15.2 cm)	White, rose, pink	Early summer to fall, but of short duration	Sun
G. paniculata (baby's-breath)	2 to 3 ft (.6 to .9 m)	White	Early summer and summer	Sun
Helenium spp. (Helen's flower)	2 to 4 ft (.6 to 1.2 m)	Orange, yellow, rusty shades	Summer, fall	Sun
Helianthus annuus (common garden sunflower)	3 to 10 ft (.9 to 3 m) PD 3 in (7.6 cm)	Yellow, orange, mahogany, or yellow with black centers	Summer	Sun
H. decapetalus x *multiflorus* (sunflower)	to 4 ft (1.2 m)	Yellow	Summer	Sun
Helichrysum bractaetum (strawflower)	2 to 4 ft (.6 to 1.2 m) PD 9 to 12 in (22.9 to 30.4 cm)	Mixed warm shades; yellow, bronze, orange, pink, white	Late summer, fall	Sun

Botanical and Common Name	Approx. Height	Range of Colors	Peak Blooming Season	Light Requirement
Hemerocallis spp. (daylily)	1 to 6 ft (.3 to 1.8 m)	Most colors except blue, green, violet, true red	Midsummer	Sun or light shade
Hesperis matronalis (sweet rocket)	2 to 3 ft (.6 to .9 m)	White, lavender	Early summer	Sun or light shade
Heuchera sanguinea (coralbells)	to 18 in (45.7 cm)	Red, pink, white	Early summer	Sun or light shade
Hosta plantaginea (plantain lily)	24 to 30 in (61 to 76.2 cm)	White flowers; yellow-green leaves	Late summer	Light shade
Iberis amara (rocket candytuft)	to 20 in (50.8 cm) PD 12 in (30.4 cm)	White	Late spring	Sun
I. sempervirens (evergreen candytuft)	8 to 12 in (20.3 to 50.8 cm)	White	Early summer	Sun or light shade
I. umbellata (globe candytuft)	12 to 18 in (50.8 to 45.7 cm) PD 16 in (40.6 cm)	Pastel pink, lavender, rose, lilac, salmon, white	Late spring	Sun
Impatiens balsamina (garden balsam)	8 to 30 in (20.3 to 76.2 cm) PD 9 in (22.9 cm)	White, pink, rose, red	Summer to fall	Light shade, sun where cool
I. walleriana (impatiens)	6 to 24 in (15.2 to 61 cm) PD 9 in (22.9 cm)	Scarlet, mauve, coral, magenta, purple, pink, white	Summer through early fall	Light shade
Iris cristata (crested iris)	6 to 8 in (15.2 to 20.3 cm)	Lavender, light blue	Spring	Light shade
I. dichotoma (vesper iris)	30 to 36 in (76.2 to 91.4 cm)	Pale lavender marked purple	Summer	Sun
I. kaempferi (Japanese iris)	to 48 in (1.2 m)	Purple, violet, pink, rose, red, white	Spring	Sun or light shade
I. spp. (bearded iris)	15 to 28 in (38.1 to 71.1 cm)	Many colors	Spring, early summer	Sun

Botanical and Common Name	Approx. Height	Range of Colors	Peak Blooming Season	Light Requirement
I. spp. (dwarf iris)	3 to 10 in (7.6 to 25.4 cm)	Many colors	Spring, early summer	Sun
Lathyrus odoratus (winter-flowering sweet pea)	3 to 6 ft (.9 to 1.8 m) PD 6 in (15.2 cm)	Mixed or separate colors; all except yellow, orange and green	Late winter where mild; not heat-resistant	Sun
L. odoratus (summer sweet pea)	3 to 6 ft (.9 to 1.8 m) PD 6 in (15.2 cm)	Mixed or separate colors; all except yellow, orange and green	Spring, where mild; early summer elsewhere. Somewhat heat-resistant	Sun
Liatris pycnostachya (gay-feather)	5 to 6 ft (1.4 to 1.8 m)	Rose-purple	Summer	Sun or light shade
Limonium bonduelii (L. sinuatum) (statice, sea-lavender)	18 to 30 in (45.7 to 76.2 cm) PD 15 in (38.1 cm)	Blue, rose, lavender, yellow, bi-colors with white	Summer	Sun
L. latifolium (statice, sea lavender)	2 to 3 ft (.6 to .9 m)	Blue, white, pink	Summer, fall	Sun
Linum grandiflorum 'Rubrum' (scarlet flax)	to 18 in (45.7 cm) PD 9 in (22.9 cm)	Scarlet to deep red, rose	Late spring, fall	Sun
L. perenne (blue flax)	20 to 24 in (50.8 to 61 cm)	Sky blue	Summer	Sun
Lithodora diffusa (lithodora)	6 to 12 in (15.2 to 30.4 cm)	Blue	Summer	Sun
Lobelia cardinalis (cardinal flower)	2 to 3 ft (.6 to .9 m)	Red	Late summer	Sun or light shade
L. erinus (lobelia)	2 to 6 in (5 to 15.2 cm) PD 6 to 8 in (15.2 to 20.3 cm)	Blue, violet, pink, white	Summer	Sun or light shade
Lobularia maritima (sweet alyssum)	to 8 in (20.3 cm) PD 12 in (30.4 cm)	White, purple, lavender, rosy pink	Year-round where mild; spring to fall elsewhere	Sun or light shade

Botanical and Common Name	Approx. Height	Range of Colors	Peak Blooming Season	Light Requirement
Lupinus hartwegii (annual lupine)	18 to 36 in (45.7 to 91.4 cm) PD 12 to 18 in (30.4 to 45.7 cm)	Blue, white	Early summer	Sun or light shade
L. polyphyllus	2 to 4 ft (.6 to 1.2 m)	Red	Summer	Sun or shade
Lythrum spp. (loosestrife)	to 5 ft (1.5 m)	Rose to purple	Summer, fall	Sun or light shade
Mathiola incana (stock)	1 to 3 ft (.3 to .9 m) PD 9 to 12 in (22.9 to 30.4 cm)	White, cream, yellow, pink, rose, crimson, red, purple	Winter where mild; late spring elsewhere	Sun
Mertensia virginica (Virginia bluebell or cowslip)	16 to 24 in (40.6 to 61 cm)	Bicolor blue	Early spring	Light shade
Mirabilis jalapa (four-o'clock)	3 to 4 ft (.9 to 1.2 m) PD 12 in (30.4 cm)	Red, yellow, pink, white; some with markings	All summer	Sun or light shade
Molucella laevis (shellflower)	18 to 30 in (45.7 to 76.2 cm) PD 9 to 12 in (22.9 to 30.4 cm)	Green, bell-like bracts resembling flowers	Summer	Sun
Monarda didyma (bee balm)	30 to 36 in (76.2 to 91.4 cm)	White, pink, scarlet red,	Summer, fall	Sun or light shade
Myosotis sylvatica (forget-me-not)	6 to 12 in (15.2 to 30.4 cm) PD 6 to 9 in (15.2 to 22.9 cm)	Blue with white eye	Spring, late fall	Light shade
Nemesia strumosa (nemesia)	to 18 in (45.7 cm) PD 9 in (22.9 cm)	All colors except green	Spring where mild; early summer elsewhere	Sun
Nicotiana alata (*N. sanderae*) (flowering tobacco)	2 to 4 ft (.6 to 1.2 m) PD 12 in (30.4 cm)	Greenish white, crimson, magenta	Summer	Sun or light shade
Nigella damascena (love-in-a-mist)	12 to 30 (30.4 to 76.2 cm) PD 9 in (22.9 cm)	Blue, white, rose-pink	Spring	Sun
Oenothera spp. (evening primrose)	2 to 6 ft (.6 to 1.8 m)	Yellow, pink	Summer	Sun

Botanical and Common Name	Approx. Height	Range of Colors	Peak Blooming Season	Light Requirement
Paeonia spp. (peony)	2 to 4 ft (.6 to 1.2 m)	White, pink crimson, lavender, cream	Early summer	Light shade
Papaver orientale (Oriental poppy)	2 to 4 ft (.6 to 1.2 m)	Pink, white, scarlet, salmon, orange	Early summer	Sun
P. rhoeas (Shirley poppy)	2 to 5 ft (.6 to 1.5 m) PD 12 in (30.4 cm)	Red, pink, white, scarlet, salmon, bi-colors	Late Summer	Sun
Pelargonium domesticum (Lady Washington geranium)	2 to 4 ft (.6 to 1.2 m)	Many bicolors; white, pink, red, purple	Summer, fall	Sun
Penstemon spp. (beard-tongue)	18 to 36 in (45.7 to 91.4 cm)	Blue, pink, crimson; mostly bicolors	Summer, fall	Sun
Petunia hybrids	to 18 in (to 45.7 cm) PD 6 to 12 in (15.2 to 30.4 cm)	All colors except true blue, yellow and orange	Summer, fall	Sun
Phlox divaricata (Sweet William phlox)	10 to 12 in (25.4 to 30.4 cm)	Blue, white, pink, rose	Early spring	Sun or light shade
P. drummondii (annual phlox)	6 to 18 in (15.2 to 45.7 cm) PD 6 to 9 in (15.2 to 22.9 cm)	Numerous bicolors; all shades except blue, gold	Late spring to fall	Sun
P. paniculata (summer perennial phlox)	3 to 5 ft (.9 to 1.5 m)	Pink, purple, rose, white, orange, red	Late summer, fall	Sun
Physalis alkekengi (Chinese-lantern)	1 to 2 ft (.3 to .6 m) PD 6 to 12 in (15.2 to 30.4 cm)	White flowers, orange bracts	Late summer	Sun or shade
Physostegia virginiana (false dragonhead)	3 to 4 ft (.9 to 1.2 m)	White and rose bicolors	Midsummer to late summer	Sun
Platycodon grandiflorum (balloon flower)	18 to 42 in (45.7 to 107 cm)	Pink, white, purple, blue	Midsummer to late summer	Sun or shade

Botanical and Common Name	Approx. Height	Range of Colors	Peak Blooming Season	Light Requirement
Polygonatum multiflorum (Solomon's-seal)	10 to 12 in (25.4 to 30.4 cm)	White	Spring	Sun or shade
Portulaca grandiflora (moss rose)	4 to 8 in (10.2 to 20.3 cm) PD 6 in (15.2 cm)	Satiny red-purple, cerise, rose-pink, white, orange, yellow	Summer	Sun
Potentilla atrosanguinea (cinquefoil)	10 to 12 (25.4 to 30.4 cm)	Red	Summer	Sun
Primula spp.	10 to 14 in (25.4 to 35.6 cm)	Bicolors; blue, red, yellow, orange, pink	Late spring, summer	Sun or shade
Pyrethum spp. (See *Chrysanthemum coccineum*)				
Reseda odorata (common mignonette)	8 to 18 in (20.3 to 45.7 cm) PD 12 in (30.4 cm)	Greenish brown clusters	Late spring to fall	Sun
Rudbeckia hirta (black-eyed Susan)	3 to 4 ft (.9 to 1.2 m)	Yellow, pink, orange, white	Summer	Sun
Salpiglossis sinuata (painted-tongue)	18 to 36 in (45. 7 to 91.4 cm) PD 9 in (22.9 cm)	Bizarre patterns of red, orange, yellow, pink, purple	Early summer	Sun or light shade
Salvia patens (blue salvia or or meadow sage)	2 to 3 ft (.6 to .9 m)	Dark blue	Summer, fall	Sun
S. splendens (scarlet sage)	10 to 36 in (25.4 to 91.4 cm) PD 18 in (45.7 cm)	Bright red, rose, lavender-pink	Summer, fall	Sun
Scabiosa atropurpurea (sweet scabiosa)	2 to 3 ft (.6 to .9 m) PD 12 in (30.4 cm)	Purple, blue, mahogany, white, rose	Summer	Sun
S. caucasica (pincushion flower)	24 to 30 in (61 to 76.2 cm)	White, blue, purple	Summer, fall	Sun
Schizanthus pinnatus (butterfly flower)	10 to 18 in (25.4 to 45.7 cm) PD 9 to 12 in (22.9 to 30.4 cm)	White, rose purple-spotted	Spring	Light shade

Botanical and Common Name	Approx. Height	Range of Colors	Peak Blooming Season	Light Requirement
Sedum sieboldii (sedum)	6 to 8 in (15.2 to 20.3 cm)	Pink, coppery foliage in fall	Late summer, fall	Sun or shade
Solidago spp. (goldenrod)	to 2 ft (.6 m)	Yellow	Summer	Sun or light shade
Tagetes erecta (hybrids and species; African or Aztec marigold)	1 to 4 ft (.3 to 1.2 m) PD 12 to 18 in (30.4 to 45.7 cm)	Mostly yellow, tangerine, and gold	Generally all summer	Sun
T. patula (hybrids and species; French marigold)	6 to 18 in (15.2 to 45.7 cm) PD 9 in (22.9 cm)	Same as African types; also russet, mahogany, and bicolors	Early summer	Sun
T. tenuifolia signata (signet marigold)	10 to 24 in (25.4 to 61 cm) PD 9 to 12 in (22.9 to 30.4 cm)	Small; yellow, orange	Generally all summer	Sun
Tithonia rotundi-folia (Mexican sunflower)	6 to 8 ft (1.8 to 2.4 m) PD 30 in (76.2 cm)	Orange	Summer	Sun
Trachymene coerulea (blue lace flower)	18 to 24 in (30.4 to 61 cm) PD 9 in (22.9 cm)	Blue to violet-blue	Late spring, early summer	Sun
Tritoma spp. (*Kniphofia* or torch lily)	2 to 6 ft (.6 to 1.8 m)	Cream, white, yellow, orange	Early summer	Sun
Tropaeolum majus (garden nasturtium)	12 to 18 in (30.4 to 45. 7 cm) PD 12 to 15 in (30.4 to 38.1 cm)	White, pink, crimson, orange, maroon, yellow	Spring and fall; summer	Sun or shade
Verbena hybrida (hortensis or garden verbena)	6 to 12 in (15.2 to 30.4 cm) PD 9 to 12 in (22.9 to 30.4 cm)	Bright pink, scarlet, blue, purple; some bicolors	Summer	Sun
Veronica spp. (speedwell)	2 to 3 ft (.6 to .9 m)	Blue, pink, white	Midsummer	Light shade
Viola cornuta (tufted pansy)	6 to 8 in (15.2 to 20.3 cm)	Purple; newer varieties in many colors	Spring, fall	Light shade

Botanical and Common Name	Approx. Height	Range of Colors	Peak Blooming Season	Light Requirement
V. tricolor 'Hortensis' (pansy)	6 to 8 in (15.2 to 20.3 cm) PD 9 in (22.9 cm)	"Faces" in white, yellow, purple, rose, mahogany, violet, apricot	Spring, fall; winter where mild	Sun
Yucca filamentosa (Adam's-needle)	3 to 6 ft (.9 to 1.8 m)	White	Late summer	Sun
Zinnia angustifolia (Mexican zinnia)	12 to 18 in (30.4 to 45.7 cm) PD 6 to 9 in (15.2 to 22. 9 cm)	Yellow, orange, white, maroon, mahogany	Summer	Sun
Z. elegans (giant-flowered zinnia)	1 to 3 ft (.3 to .9 m) PD 12 in (30.4 cm)	Red, orange, yellow, purple, pink, white	Summer	Sun
Z. elegans (small-flowered zinnia)	1 to 3 ft (.3 to .9 m) PD 9 in (22.9 cm)	Red, orange, yellow, purple, lavender, pink, white	Summer	Sun

(PD—Planting Distance)

Chapter Eight

CONTAINER GARDENING

*W*hen plants are in containers and planter boxes, they can be watered easily and moved about easily to where you want them at any time. Trees, shrubs, bulbs and various other plants can all thrive within the confines of a decorative container or a wooden planter box. The standard pots and tubs are perfect for a rustic or cottage look; the formal look of planter boxes is well suited to contemporary homes.

CONTAINERS

The standard terra cotta container is available in many variations. The attractive *Italian pots* have a modified border and have rounded, beveled or rimless edges. The formal *Venetian pots* are barrel shaped with a band design pressed into the sides. *Spanish pots* have sides that slope outward and flared lips. These are good containers for many plants. *Cylindrical pots* are straight from top to bottom. *Bulb pans* or *seed bowls* are shallow but have drainage holes. The *azalea* or *fern pot* is a squat container. It is in better proportion to most plants than conventional contain-

The standard terra cotta pot is available in sizes from small to large. (Photo by Jack Kramer)

ers. *Three-legged pots* are bowl shaped. *Donkey* or *chicken containers* are novelty pots with pockets for soil. *Strawberry jars* have pockets for side plantings.

Other containers come in plastic, ceramic, wood and stone. Plastic pots are lightweight, making them liable to tip over when large plants are placed in them. The pots come in all sizes and shapes and in many colors. Because they are nonporous, they hold water longer than do terra cotta containers.

Ceramic containers are quite attractive and come in endless colors and patterns. They have separate saucers or the saucer directly attached to the container. *Cachepots*—decorative ceramic pots—have no drainage holes. Both plastic and ceramic containers are also available as hanging pots.

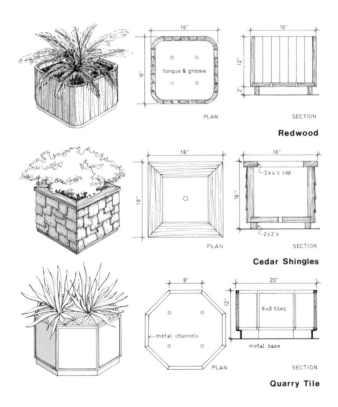

Figure 8.1—Portable Planters (Adrián Martínez)

Round, square or hexagonal wood tubs may need a preservative coating. Ornamental stone or concrete tubs are even heavier when filled with soil. Tapered stone bowls are very striking when filled with flowering plants.

Wooden boxes can be perfect cubes; cubes, detailed or plain. Redwood is the best material because it needs no preservatives and lasts for years. Douglas fir is even stronger, but it needs a protective coating. You may have to build your own boxes (see Figure 8.1). Small boxes (3 inches [7.6 cm] deep, good for bulbs and annuals) and medium ones (fine for shrubs) should be made of 1-inch-thick (2.5-cm-thick) wood. Large planters (24 inches [61 cm] long, for trees) should be constructed of 2-inch-thick (5-cm-thick) boards. Glue or nail the boards together. Make sure the bottom boards are spaced 1/4 inch (.6 cm) apart, so water can drain out.

PLANTING

Most plants thrive on a mixture of 2 parts garden loam, 1 part sand and 1 part leafmold and bonemeal. Begonias and ferns need 2 parts garden loam, 2 parts sand and 2 parts leafmold. Bulbs use 3 parts garden loam, 1 part sand and 1 part leafmold. Cacti and succulents grow best in 2 parts garden loam, 2 parts sand and 1 part leafmold and limestone. If you are growing bromeliads and orchids, use 1 part medium-grade fir bark and 1 part chopped osmunda.

In containers, put broken pieces of pots or crushed stone in for drainage. In wood planters, lay in a bed of small stones or chipped gravel and then scatter some charcoal over the bed. Now spread your soil over your drainage pieces or the planter bed. Make sure your plants are in proportion to their containers or boxes.

WATERING AND FEEDING

After they have been planted, water plants thoroughly. Container plants dry out faster than in-ground plants because they are more exposed to the elements. All waterings after the first planting should be heavy; too little water will create waterlogged pockets of soil. Thus, water plants thoroughly, but then let them become somewhat dry before the next watering. Hose the foliage to remove any hidden insects. To feed contained plants, use a commercial soluble fertilizer 10-10-5, but dilute it more than the

Containers can also be terrace beds; the saw-tooth design is distinctive.

directions indicate. Also, feed more often than the bottle instructs. Most large plants in large containers or boxes should be fed about four times in the summer, those in smaller pots or boxes about once a month during the growing season. Do not feed sick or newly potted plants, and never feed in winter. Apply light solutions once in early spring and once in fall.

PLANTS FOR CONTAINER GARDENING

Annuals, perennials, bulbs, trees, shrubs—all are ideal candidates for containers and wood planter boxes. Annuals have shallow roots, and their colors are outstanding. Petunias, rain lilies, balsam, lobelia, browallia, cineraria, impatiens and primrose provide constant summer color. Feed annuals biweekly. Water them heavily on warm days, and place them where they will receive some sunshine.

Geraniums, tuberous begonias, chrysanthemums, hosta and lantana are excellent perennials. All perennials must rest during the year at some time. Summer-blooming perennials rest over the winter; winter-blooming perennials rest in summer.

Good bulbs for containers and planter boxes include achemines, autumn crocus, daffodils, hyacinths and Kaffir lilies. You can plant spring bulbs in the fall and store them through the winter in a cool dark spot. Bring them indoors in early winter; move them outside when the weather stays warm. Outdoors, after bulbs flower, keep the foliage on and bring the bulbs inside. Let them keep growing until leaves begin yellowing; then let the soil dry. Store the bulbs—remove them from their pot or planter box—in paper sacks in a cool spot. Plant the bulbs in the following fall.

To start bulbs in the soil mix we recommend covering the bottom of the pot or box with pebbles. Fill one-third of the pot or box with soil. Set the bulbs on top of the soil. Fill in and around the bulbs with soil until their tips are barely covered.

Small trees provide shade and visual interest. Square or rectangular boxes are best for trees with bold foliage. Small trees are sold at nurseries in 5-, 10-, or 15-gallon (18.9, 37.8 or 56.8 l) cans, in fast- or slow-growing kinds. In areas with harsh winters, determine where you will store the trees during freezing temperatures. Good locations are a garage, a basement or an enclosed porch. Grow hardy trees and shrubs in climates with severe winters.

Annuals for the Container Garden

The following annuals will thrive in containers and planter boxes.

Browallia speciosa—a spring- and summer-blooming annual with amethyst flowers.

Cineraria—does well in partial shade and cool conditions; has blue, purple, crimson, white and red flowers.

Impatiens—these annuals need sunlight and feeding; numerous varieties have many different colors, including pink, white and lavender.

Lobelia—these blue flowers bloom through the summer and fall.

Petunias—these are easy-to-grow annuals that need sunlight and water; varieties come in dwarf, trailing and ruffled types, in white, purple, red, lavender, pink and yellow.

Primrose—do better in some shade—the flowers are pink, lavender or white.

Perennials for the Container Garden

These perennials will flourish in containers and planter boxes.

Acanthus mollis (Grecian urn)—this perennial needs little care; it has erect spikes of white and lilac flowers in green bracts.

Campanula isophylla (Italian bellflower)—this small plant has blue star-shaped flowers and needs an ornate container and much water and partial shade.

Chrysanthemum—give these plants sunlight (but some varieties bloom in partial shade) and keep soil fairly wet; flowers come in many colors, and many varieties bloom as late as November (pinch back plants early in the season).

Geranium—'Lady Washington' varieties have pink, red, lavender or white flowers with and without markings; the garden geranium is *Pelargonium hortorum*, with single or double flowers in white, pink, red or salmon.

Hellebore—several species are good for boxes and tubs: Christmas rose, *Helleborus niger*, and Lenten rose, *H. orientalis*.

Hosta (plantain lily)—this easy-to-grow perennial is good in difficult areas because it often blooms in dense shade.

Lantana—these strong, hard-to-kill plants need full sunlight and rather dry soil; trailing lantania (*Lantana montevidensis*), with purple flowers, is ideal in hanging baskets.

Bulbs for the Container Garden

The following bulbs will provide vivid color for the container garden.

Achimenes—all achimenes need sunlight and copious amounts of water; the flowers come in various colors.

Autumn crocus—do well in wet soil and partial shade; flowers are brilliant yellow, lavender or rose and bloom in August and September.

Daffodil—prefer sunshine and a fair amount of water; bloom from January to May.

Hyacinth—need a lot of sunlight and water; the fragrant flowers come in white, pink or blue and bloom in March and April.

Kaffir lily—these spring-blooming plants have dramatic clusters of vivid orange or red flowers.

Shrubs and Trees for the Container Garden

These shrubs and trees will provide dramatic accents in the container garden.

Abutilon (flowering maple).

Acer circinatum (vine maple)—lovely autumn color.

Aeonium arboreum—with ornamental leaf rosettes; this plant grows well in shallow containers.

Agave attenuata (century plant)—thrives for many years in a large tub.

Aloe arborescens—spiny leaves and beautiful winter blooms.

Araucaria heterophylla—dark green horizontal branches in symmetrical designs.

Aucuba japonica (Japanese aucuba)—shiny ovate or oblong dark green leaves.

Azalea, Kurume—dense, striking foliage; the plant blooms profusely.

Bambusa (bamboo)—woody grasses with variations in stem color.

B. sempervirens (common boxwood)—shiny dark green leaves, dense foliage.

Camellia japonica—wonderful container plant.

C. sasanqua—shiny green leaves; profuse white blooms in autumn.

Cedrus deodara (deodar cedar)—dark bluish green leaves.

Chaenomeles 'Contorta' (flowering quince)—twisted and contorted branches; blooms in early spring.

Chamaedorea elegans—feathery leaves.

Crataegus phaenopyrum (Washington hawthorn)—white flowers; red berries in winter; beautiful fall color.

Dioon edule—feathery leaves; thrives in sunshine.

Elaeagnus pungens (silverberry)—likes a sunny location.

Fagus sylvatica (European beech)—shiny dark green leaves turn reddish brown in autumn.

F. sylvatica 'Purpurea-pendula'—striking weeping beech; thrives for years in a large pot.

Fatshedera lizei—shiny green leaves resembling giant ivy.

Fatsia japonica 'Moseri'—glossy bold leaves.

Ficus benjamina (fig)—broad, with graceful branches.

Gardenia jasminoides (Cape jasmine)—thick leaves. Plants need a warm atmosphere.

Ginkgo biloba (maidenhair tree)—beautiful brilliant yellow leaves in the fall.

Juniperus chinensis 'Torulosa' (Chinese juniper)—twisted branches.

Larus nobilis (sweet bay)—dark and glossy green leaves.

Ligustrum lucidum (glossy privet)—thick leathery leaves and small white flowers.

Osmanthus fragrans—fragrant white flowers.

Phormium tenax (New Zealand flax)—grows quite large and thrives even when neglected.

Phyllostachys nigra (black-jointed bamboo)—green and black stems; unsurpassed for an oriental motif.

P. viridiglaucescens—attractive yellow stems.

Picea glauca 'Conica'—symmetrical appearance.

Pieris japonica (Japanese andromeda)—drooping flower clusters year-round.

Pinus thunbergiana (Japanese black pine)—this slow-growing tree has uneven, upright branches.

Pittosporum phillyaeoides (narrow-leaved pittosporum)—this plant, with drooping branchlets, grows well in a sunny location.

P. undulatum (Victorian box)—fragrant blossoms.

Podocarpus macrophyllus 'Maki'—small leaves.

Prunus x *blirieana* (cherry plum)—red-purple foliage.

P. serrulata—striking clustered flowers that bloom in spring.

Rhapis excelsa—fanlike leaves.

Rhododendron 'Brick-a-Brac'—white blossoms in the winter; a low-growing plant.

Rosa (rose)—plant in large containers because roots should not be cramped.

Tsuga canadensis 'Pendula' (Canada hemlock)—weeping branches; slow growing.

Chapter Nine

Small Gardens in the City

*T*rellises, planter boxes and containers now enable city dwellers to enjoy the delights of gardening—even on their rooftops! You can re-landscape or start fresh with shrubs, trees, vines and other attractive plants in the backyard, in doorways or on the terrace.

BACKYARDS

The backyard can be a path with flower beds or a patio. In any event, before you turn the area into your personal gardening statement, decide exactly what kind of garden you want and the mood you want to impart. Then consider your conditions: sun, shade, wind and so on. A single dominant theme is

Rooftop gardens are usually small, so taking advantage of the space is necessary. Here we have a working area, potting shed, arbor and container garden. (Photo by Matthew Barr)

the easiest idea with which to work. To integrate the garden and your building, have both planting beds and paved areas. Consider these areas before you do any planting. You should have a minimum of paths. Paving stones or cross sections of tree trunks (rounds) create a design that monotonous straight paths do not. Also consider borders for paths and flower beds of brick, concrete or stone as other accents. Fences and walls, for privacy and decoration, are also necessary. However, fences higher than 6 feet (1.8 m) are formidable and out of scale. A canopy or trellis is nice in backyards, but a tree is just as effective.

You will need raised beds for plantings if the soil is bad. Raised beds add depth to the soil and elevate plants to a height where viewers can better see them. Construct raised beds of fieldstone or mortar walls, or use brick or redwood planters.

Be sure plants are healthy and attractive. Use some other outdoor feature, such as a bench or a fountain, to complement plants. Locate such items in the rear of the garden near a fence or in a corner, so they stand out. The outdoor feature should blend with the yard and be the focal point of the garden.

Group containers of geraniums or chrysanthemums for color in patio corners, in rows, along paths or near fences. Annuals look good in low redwood boxes. Bulbs supply spring and summer color, and evergreens provide winter accent. Suitable plants for backyard gardens

Having a special place for plants—no matter how small—opens new avenues of gardening. (Photo by Jack Kramer)

are azaleas, flowering quince, white dogwood, mountain laurel, rock cotoneaster, hemlock, Japanese holly, Japanese maple, dwarf boxwood, firethorn, climbing roses and Boston ivy.

DOORWAYS

Doorways can and should be hospitable welcoming locations. Matching ceramic containers brimming with foliage plants are simple yet graceful. The height and mass of the plants should be in proportion to the size of the door. If the doorway has entry steps, use matching tubs filled with plants that have mass and foliage. However, the plants should not obstruct foot traffic.

At a formal entrance porch with a roof, use low and round box hedges in front, with a pair of large white boxes. Antique urns filled with flowers and set on brick platforms are graceful and charming. In a very plain entrance, a long redwood planter box filled with foliage plants gently leads visitors from outdoors to indoors.

A single specimen plant in a handsome jardiniere by the side of the door is a dramatic welcome. Ivy, fatshedera and ginkgo are all good plants for doorways.

TERRACES

Terraces, like doorways, must be carefully planned. Because of the limited space, place small trees in corners. One small container tree, such as a Japanese maple, is good accent. Attach plants to walls and use hanging baskets wherever possible. Windowboxes work well if the terrace has a railing or a parapet.

Shrubs and Trees for the City Garden

The following trees and shrubs will thrive in a city garden.

DECIDUOUS TREES
  Betula alba (white birch)
  Carpinus betulus (European hornbeam)
  Cornus florida (flowering dogwood)
  Crataegus oxyacantha (English hawthorn)
  C. phaenopyrum (Washington hawthorn)
  Ginkgo biloba (maidenhair tree)
  Ilex opaca (American holly)

Magnolia glauca
(swamp magnolia)
M. soulangeana (saucer
magnolia)
M. stellata (star
magnolia)
Malus spp.(flowering
crab apples)
Prunus serrulata
(Japanese flowering
cherry)
Sophora japonica
(Japanese pagoda tree)
Styrax japonicus
(snowbell tree)
Syringa pekinensis
(Pekingnese lilac)
Ulmus pumila (dwarf
Asiatic elm)

EVERGREEN TREES

Pinus mugo (mountain
pine)
P. sylvestris (Scots
pine)
Taxus cuspidata
'Capitata' (Japanese
yew)
Thuja occidentalis
(American arborvitae)

DECIDUOUS SHRUBS

*Acanthopanaz
pentaphyllum* (fiveleaf
aralia)
Azalea spp.
Berberis thunbergii
(Japanese barberry)
Deutzia scabra (rough
deutzia)
Forsythia spp.
Hibiscus syriacus (rose-
of-Sharon)
Lagerstroemia indica
(crape myrtle)

Ligustrum ibota (ibota
privet)
L. ovalifolium
(California privet)
Myrica carolinensis
(bayberry)
Nandina domestica
(heavenly bamboo)
Philadelphus (mock
orange)
Rhus cotinus
(smokebush)
Spiraea vanhouttei
(Vanhoutte's spirea)
*Symphoricarpos
vulgaris* (snowberry)
Syringa vulgaris
(lilac)
Vitex agnus-castus
(chaste tree)
Weigela (hybrids;
weigela)

EVERGREEN SHRUBS

*Buxus microphylla
koreana* (Korean
boxwood)
Ilex crenata (Japanese
holly)
Kalmia latifolia
(mountain laurel)
*Osmanthus
heterophyllus* (holly
olive)
Pieris japonica
(Japanese andromeda)
Pyracantha coccinea
(firethorn)
*Rhododendron
carolinianum*
(Carolina rhododen-
dron)
R. mucronulatum
(snow azalea)
R. hybrids

✿
SPECIAL GARDENS
FOR SMALL AREAS

*E*ven in the small garden it is possible to have a special section of herbs, vegetables or even roses. Indeed, the herb and vegetable garden can be grown in a 5- by 10-foot (1.5-x-3-m) area and provide enough seasonings and greens for the average family all summer. A rose garden can—with clever design—be done on a diminutive scale.

Plan these gardens carefully; use every inch of available space. Although they may not be as grandiose as their larger counterparts, they offer great satisfaction to the homeowner.

HERB GARDENS

Herb gardens were once patterned upon somewhat intricate lines. Today's herb garden is much less formal. The layout is generally a simple one and can be put in place over a single weekend. Some planning is necessary, but elaborate designs are not needed. Yet for all its simplicity, the herb garden can be a delightful scene of foliage textures and colors joining with flower form and gentle color.

The small herb garden close to the kitchen is, of course, a convenience. Or the garden can be used as an accent away from the house; here, of course, a more formal design might be needed. But no matter where you put the garden, choose a sunny place, because herbs do not do well in shaded areas. The garden should be neat and weeded, with paths and some borders to set it off in the landscape. A good background, such as a wall or fence or even a hedge, helps too.

The garden design can take many shapes—wagonwheel, butterfly, knot—and the garden can have herbs for fragrance, flavor and medicinal uses. Herbs are divided into several groups, although there is some overlapping. Those grown for fragrance are known as aromatic herbs; culinary herbs are used for cooking and seasoning; medicinal herbs have an infinite variety of uses. There is special charm in a herb garden, and it is a delight to be able to pick your own seasonings.

Select a well-drained site for the herb garden; a place with a slight slope is good, so that water will not stand around plant crowns. Most herbs prefer a neutral or slightly alkaline soil, so, if your soil is acid, apply liberal amounts of lime to the garden each spring. Be sure the site has plenty of sun; eight hours daily is ideal, but most herbs will (if necessary) tolerate only four hours.

To prepare the garden, stake out the area with string and stakes. Remove any debris, large stones and weeds. Work the soil until it is porous and crumbly. Dig down at least 12 to 18 inches (30.4 to 45.8 cm) and prepare the ground carefully so the plants will thrive. Do not attempt to plant in dry clay soils, or the herbs will die.

Hardy perennial herbs are bought as young plants, and annuals and biennials are started yearly from seed. Put perennials in the ground in spring, and, when frost danger is over, sow seed for the annuals and biennials. Sprinkle the seeds over prepared soil and then cover with a light layer of soil. Moisten thoroughly with a fine mist.

Germination of seed varies with the herb, so don't panic if some herbs take a long time to sprout. Keep the plants reasonably moist during this time. Most seeds should be planted in the spring, but herbs such as thyme, dill and parsley can be sown in summer too. Herbs should be cut just as the flowers are about to open and when the essential oils are most abundant.

Herbs for Fragrance

These aromatic herbs add fragrance and spice to the small garden.

Basil (*Ocimum minimum*)

Bergamot (*Monarda*)

    Monarda didyma (bee balm)

Geranium (*Pelargonium*)

    Pelargonium crispum (citronella geranium)

    P. denticulatum (skeleton geranium)

    P. graveolens (rose geranium)

P. limoneum (lemon geranium)

P. melissinum (balm geranium)

P. odoratissimum (apple geranium)

Lavender (*Lavandula*)

    Lavandula dentata (French lavender)

    L. spica (English lavender)

    L. vera (English lavender)

Lavender cotton (*Santolina chamaecyparissus*)

Lemon verbena (*Lippia Citriodora*)

Marjoram (*Organum*)

Mint (*Mentha*)

    Mentha citrata (orange mint)

    M. crispa (curled mint)

    M. rotundifolia (apple mint)

Rosemary (*Rosmarinus officinalis*)

Rue (*Ruta graveolens*)

Savory (*Satureja*)

    Satureja hortensis (summer savory)

    S. montana (winter savory)

Southernwood (*Artemisia abrotanum*)

Thyme (*Thymus*)

Woodruff, sweet (*Asperula odorata*)

Herbs for the Small Garden

The following herbs will provide variety and attractive foliage to the small garden.

Anise (A)
(Pimpinella anisum)

Balm (P)
(lemon balm)
(Melissa officinalis)

Basil (A)
(Ocimum minimum)

Basil, sweet (A)
(Ocimum basilicum)

Bergamot (P)
(Monarda fistulosa)

Borage (A)
(Borago officinalis)

Chamomile (P)
(Anthemis nobilis,
Matricaria chamomilla)

Chervil (A)
(Anthriscus
cerefolium)

Chives (P)
(Allium
schoenoprasum)

Coriander (A)
(Coriandrum sativum)

Cumin (A)
(Cuminum cyminum)

Dill (A)
(Anethum graveolens)

Fennel, sweet (A)
(Foeniculum
officinale)

Fennel flower (A)
(Nigella sativa)

Flag, sweet (P)
(Acorus calamus)

Geranium, scented by
variety (P)
(Pelargonium)

Horseradish (P)
(Armoracia rusticana)

Lavender (P)
    (English lavender)
    (Lavandula spica,
L. vera)
    (French lavender)
    (L. dentata)

Lavender cotton (P)
(Santolina
chamaecyparissus)

Lemon verbena (P)
(Lippia citriodora)

Lovage (P)
(Levisticum officinale)

Marjoram, sweet (A)
(Organum majorana)

Mint, apple (P)
    (apple mint)
    (Mentha
    rotundifolia)
    (curled mint)
    (M. crispa)

Parsley (B)
(Petroselinum
hortense)

Peppermint (P)
(Mentha piperita)

Rosemary (P)
(Rosmarinus
officinalis)

Rue (P)
(Ruta graveolens)

Saffron (P)
(Crocus sativus)

Sage (P)
(Salvia officinalis)

Savory (P)
    (summer savory)
    (Satureja hortensis)
    (winter savory)
    (S. montana)

Sorrel (P)
(Rumex acetosa)

Southernwood (P)
(Artemisia abrotanum)

Spearmint (P)
(Mentha spicata)

Tansy (P)	Watercress (P)
(*Tanacetum vulgare*)	(*Nasturtium-aquaticum*)
Tarragon (P)	Woodruff, sweet (P)
(*Artemisia dracunculus*)	(*Asperula odorata*)
Thyme (P)	
(*Thymus*)	Key: A Annual, B Biennial, P Perennial

ROSE GARDENS

Roses are popular flowers with a romance of their own. They have been with us for a very long time and continue to be admired and grown. A well-designed rose garden is indeed a stunning sight.

In planning this garden choose a place that has some air circulation, but is still protected from the wind. Try to select a neutral background so that the roses will be seen to their best advantage, and decide upon a definite pattern for the beds.

Roses need a fertile, well-drained, slightly acid soil with a pH ranging from 5.5 to 6.5. Because rose roots are long, dig deeply, to about 20 inches (50.8 cm). Take out an additional 3 to 6 inches (7.6 to 15.2 cm), and replace with cinders or crushed stone to ensure good drainage facilities. Roses will grow in either clay or sandy soil, but they will not thrive unless drainage is almost perfect and the soil is fertile.

For good rose blooms, be sure the garden is in a sunny spot; roses need about five hours of sun daily. Some shade is beneficial in the afternoon.

In the first season of growth, feeding may not be necessary if the original planting was done with care. In the second year start a fertilization program; roses are heavy feeders and need nitrogen, phosphorus and potash. Give them at least two or three feedings a year: the first in spring soon after pruning, the second in June before bloom, and the third in summer. I use a 5-10-5 fertilizer for roses, but check in your area to see what is being used with most success. Be sure the soil is moist when applying fertilizer and work it into the soil around plants with a rake.

Roses may be planted in the autumn or in the early spring. Be sure the crown of the plant is one to two inches below the soil surface. Pack soil firmly around the roots; avoid loose planting. Water evenly throughout the growing season, and do give them deep soakings rather than frequent light sprinklings. Don't give them overhead watering, since it can cause black spots to form on the foliage.

Pruning depends upon the type of rose and the locality, but there are some general rules to remember. Remove dead or weak wood and maintain the desired height. Use sharp pruning shears and make a slant cut above a vigorous bud. To guard against fungi, treat the ends of cut stems with a fungicide.

The amount of winter protection depends on the weather in your locality and the type of rose; check in your area for this information.

PLANTING AND CARE

Planting distances depend upon the type of rose. For hybrid and tea roses a distance of 18 to 24 inches (45.7 to 61 cm) apart is fine. Floribundas and grandifloras need more space—about 18 to 36 inches (45.7 to 91.4 cm) between each plant. Trim the roses before you plant them, and remove broken or injured roots. As mentioned, plant roses deep and place them in position, so that the crown (point of union between the stock and scion) is between 1 to 2 inches (2.5 to 5 cm) below the surface of the soil. In mild climates the bud union should be just above the surface of the soil. After planting, pack the soil firmly around the roots and keep the roses well watered the first few weeks until they are established.

Roses need pruning to produce strong roots and shoots; without proper cutting they get leggy and dense. In spring before growth starts, prune plants just above a node (bud); cut in a slanting direction and leave three to five buds on each stem. Only light pruning is needed for rambler roses that bloom on old wood. The ramblers that bloom on new wood from the base of the plant need pruning after flowering.

The planting time depends upon your climate. In cold areas, early spring is best for setting out dormant bushes. In the midpart of the country, early spring or late fall is suggested, and in all-year climates, roses can be planted from November to January. Bare-root plants are most often selected by gardeners. These are dormant and ready to start a new cycle of growth when you get them.

If you cannot plant roses immediately, keep them cool and be sure the roots are kept moist. Never allow rose roots to become dry before they are planted. Put them in water until you get the plants in the ground. Packaged roses are often seen, and, if they have been stored in a cool place, they are satisfactory. If the branches look dry and shriveled, chances are they have been kept in a hot location, so don't buy them. Roses grown in containers are already started for you and cost more than dormant ones, but for beginners these are the best buy.

In cold regions, plants should be protected for the winter. Place mounds of soil about 10 inches (25.4 cm) high around them. Do not scoop the soil from around the plant; rather, bring in fresh soil. Remove the covering gradually in spring when growth starts.

ROSE VARIETIES

Because there are so many roses available, first decide what kind you want. The following list should help you.

Hybrid teas have a sturdy growing habit and are hardy in the north if given suitable winter protection. They give generous bloom from June to September. Some varieties grow over 3 feet (.9 m), others are low growers. There is a wide range of color and form.

Floribunda varieties vary greatly in size; some are almost dwarf and others grow to 6 feet (1.8 m). Flower form is single to semi-double in a wide range of colors. These plants are very floriferous and less demanding than most roses.

Grandifloras are very vigorous, free-blooming and easy to grow. The flowers are borne in clusters and last very well.

Edging roses are dwarf, generally of the *polyantha* group. They are very hardy and give generous bloom throughout the season.

Hedge roses are quick growing, tall and bushy; they require very little care.

Old-fashioned roses generally have single flowers and include old favorites, such as provence rose and the damask rose.

Climbing roses can be trained to supports; some are rampant, but others are more restrained in growth; some have a peak season of bloom while others flower intermittently throughout the season. A few varieties are very hardy, but others are suitable only for mild climates.

Chapter Eleven

BASIC MAINTENANCE

*L*andscaping demands basic needs—composts, fertilizer, pruning and tools and equipment. An understanding of these needs helps you to keep your property looking good; once you have invested time, labor and money, it is senseless to have insects ruin the scheme or have plants die from lack of nutrients. Pruning trees and shrubs is necessary, too. Usually a gardener neglects his grounds because he lacks implements, so keep tools on hand.

COMPOSTS

Good soil is necessary to grow any plant successfully, and the stuff it is made of is compost. This is decomposing organic matter that you can stockpile on your grounds to improve soil. Preparing compost is working with nature; it involves leaves, lawn clippings, old plants, small twigs and food scraps in a small pile. Have the compost heap in an inconspicuous but accessible place; the area does not have to be larger than 5 square feet (.46 sq. m). I use 2-foot by 4-foot (.6-x-1.2-m) boards on three sides to keep the compost heap in place and to help hide it.

Add manure and lime to the compost as you collect it. The wastes are turned into compost by bacteria, fungi and other microscopic or minute organisms. Moisture is necessary to promote decomposition, but use reasonable amounts of water; the material should not be too wet or too dry. Allow air to permeate the vegetable wastes so that decomposition takes place, and occasionally poke holes into the compost with a rake handle. Try to turn the compost now and then and keep the pile concave so that it will catch water.

Put leaves, lawn trimmings, weeds, nonwoody prunings, annual and perennial remains, banana skins and so forth in the pile. (Do not put evergreen leaves, pine shavings or sawdust into it.)

When the materials have decomposed, the compost will be black or dark brown. Decomposition time depends on climate, material used and other variables.

MULCHES

Mulching is using peat moss, salt hay, leaves or any available similar material—such as fir bark (potting medium for orchids) or a prepared mulch like Ko-Ko-O (dry outer shell of cocoa bean)—to give plants winter protection. Apply the mulch to the surface of the soil around the plants to prevent loss of soil moisture by evaporation and to keep weeds down. Use a mulch that is coarse enough to admit water, but not retain too much moisture.

When you use mulch, you are giving plants more than warmth; you are protecting them against alternating thawing and freezing, cold winds and winter sunlight. Mulching also reduces the depth to which frost penetrates, and although it cannot totally prevent erosion, it helps somewhat. Mulch can be from 2 to 5 inches (5 to 12.7 cm) deep, but do not apply it until the top few inches of the soil are frozen.

FERTILIZERS

After a while plants deplete soil of nutrients, so feeding is necessary. Do not confuse fertilizers with soil conditioners that help to keep soil porous and crumbly. Plants obtain many elements from the soil, but the three most important are nitrogen, phosphorus and potassium. Nitrogen produces good leaf and stem growth with rich green color; phosphorus promotes root development and helps to ripen tissues; potassium gives plants vigor and helps them to ward off diseases.

There are inorganic fertilizers—minerals and synthetic minerals—and organic fertilizers—manure, bone meal, dried blood, peat, etc. It is necessary to use a combination of both types to maintain and balance the sources of plant nutrition.

Complete fertilizers provide nitrogen, phosphorus and potassium in varying proportions. A 5-10-5 fertilizer has five pounds available nitrogen, ten pounds phosphoric acid and five pounds potash to each one hundred pounds.

There are dozens of fertilizers. Some are for lawns; others are for evergreens, roses and so forth. The labels on the package tell you how much to use per square foot, and it is best not to overdo it.

Digging up soil will show the tilth and condition of old soil; this soil is as porous and mealy as it should be. Some new topsoil will be added to it to give it more nutrients. (Photo USDA)

After feeding, water the plants so that nutrients penetrate the soil. Wash leaves and stems so that they will not get burned by the chemicals. Spread fertilizers evenly and thinly; don't pile them in a heap. Feed trees and shrubs by sprinkling fertilizer on the ground or by boring holes in the soil to about 18 inches (45.7 cm) and filling with fertilizers.

PRUNING

It is important to learn to prune properly for successful gardening. It helps to shape plants, promote growth and contribute to the general appearance of the landscape. Storm-broken branches and overgrown shrubs are easily seen in winter when foliage is gone. Prune out dead branches or infected and diseased limbs immediately to preserve and protect the health of the plant.

Use clean, sharp tools to cut cleanly. Apply wound paint to heavy trees and shrubs after pruning. The amount of cutting varies with different plants and their stage of development. Young shade trees must be pruned so that they will have strong frameworks. Cut out crossed branches and strive to keep the tree in an attractive shape. Cut branches flush with the trunk; there should be no stubs. Do not prune when wood is frozen or brittle.

Large shade trees with heavy branches should be handled by a professional; it is too risky to climb ladders and wrestle with heavy limbs.

Shrubs that flower on branches from previous years can be pruned immediately after they bloom in the spring or summer. Cut away weak shoots and awkward branches. Let light and air circulate so that the tree or shrub will have strong growth and flowering branches for the following seasons. Shrubs that flower on current branches need pruning in the winter or very early spring. Cut them back drastically.

Use discretion when pruning shrubs grown for ornamental fruit. Remove only dead branches, and otherwise just thin out the plant in early spring. It is best not to prune evergreen shrubs like boxwood.

Fruit trees need pruning in very late winter or in early spring. Young trees need only light cutting. Mature trees should be kept moderate in height, so that they are easy to spray and harvest.

Species roses need thinning after flowering in the summer; cut away weak and old branches. Cut climbers and ramblers at the same time, but leave as many strong new canes as possible. Prune hybrid teas in the spring; cut away dead, weak wood and crowded stems.

PRUNING GUIDELINES

Follow these rules for pruning:

1. After making a cut, apply wound paint (available at hardware stores).

2. Do not leave stubs; infection can enter.

3. Prune from the ground whenever possible.

4. Cut away crossed branches on small trees.

5. Do not let a main trunk divide into a fork; remove one branch.

6. Cut away dead limbs, for they are an invitation to rot and disease.

7. Don't cut a heavy limb with one cut because it will pull the bark from the tree. Make three cuts at different places.

8. Prune just slightly above a bud.

9. Always wear gloves, and use sharp, clean tools.

TOOLS AND EQUIPMENT

Basic tools—trowel, spading fork, spade, rake, hoe—are necessities. For watering you need one or two good garden hoses, an oscillating sprinkler, a nozzle and a watering can. For removing weeds and general cutting, keep on hand a good, sharp butcher knife, plant scissors, heavy-duty pruner, mower and hedge clippers. For moving soil and large plants, have a wheelbarrow or some sort of garden cart.

Special tools and equipment and power mowers are not necessary for smaller sites. Don't stock a cabinet of fertilizers; wait until you need them, and then buy them from your local nursery. They know what is going on in gardening in your area and will recommend the appropriate items.

⚘

Chapter Twelve

PESTS
AND DISEASES

You will never win the war against pests and blight, but you can keep trouble to a minimum by being observant and by using safe controls (including natural predators such as birds and insects) when necessary. Inspect stems and leaves frequently to be sure that pests aren't getting a foothold, for once entrenched, they are tough to get rid of. If you see them massing for an attack, however, insects still can be eradicated without resorting to strong poisons.

NATURAL PREVENTATIVES

Once we had to rely on dangerous chemicals and insect preventatives to keep our gardens healthy. Fortunately, this is not so today. There are dozens of ways to maintain a pest-free garden. Botanical repellents are a good main line of defense. Old-fashioned remedies such as soap and water are also safe ways to thwart trouble with pests. Predatory insects and birds can be effective against harmful plant critters.

BOTANICAL REPELLENTS

For the most part, botanical insecticides are safe to use in the garden. These preventatives are derived from natural plants and are not persistent or harmful to man or land. They include pyrethrum, rotenone, ryania, quassia and hellebore.

Pyrethrum is derived from a species of chrysanthemum that at one time was referred to as an insect flower. The plant has daisy-like pink or white flowers, which when pulverized are toxic to such insects as aphids, white flies, leafhoppers and thrips.

Rotenone comes from derris root, a woody climber with purple and white flowers. When ground into a powder it is effective against aphids, spider mites, chinch bugs and other pests.

Ryania is a woody Latin American shrub. The ground roots and stems are used to make a deterrent against certain destructive beetles. The quassia root, a plant from South America, is prepared in the same manner and is effective against several insects.

Finally, there is hellebore, a common garden flower whose pulverized rhizomes contain helleborin, which has a burning acidic taste and effectively wards off many insects.

Chemical companies that previously used persistent and very dangerous chemicals to fight insects have now started to produce natural preventatives in spray and pellet form. Actually, you can dry your chrysanthemum leaves and grow some of the other plants to make your own defensive arsenal without spending money on commercial products.

OLD-FASHIONED REMEDIES

Nobody likes to hand pick insects, but if you can bring yourself to touch the critters, this is still a very good way to get rid of garden pests. Many insects can be loosened by gently shaking the tree or plant. Aphids are particularly bothersome in gardens, but a 1-pound (453.6-g) bar of laundry soap (not detergent) mixed with 2 quarts (1.9 l) water and applied directly to the insects will efficiently rid the plants of aphids. This also works on mealybugs, red spiders and scale, but don't expect immediate results. It takes several applications using a standard spray bottle to really eliminate all insects, but it is worth the trouble because it creates no danger to you or the environment.

Another good deterrent against bugs (and one I have used for years) is standard rubbing alcohol. Apply the alcohol on cotton swabs directly to the pest. It is not diffcult to apply and works very well—far better than dubious chemicals.

PREDATORY INSECTS

Insects are not all bad; indeed, there are predatory insects (available through various mail-order suppliers) that keep the balance of nature and your garden in order. Generally, most people do not want to mess with these insects and some believe that the insects simply disperse after their introduction into the garden. This may be true, but if there are prey insects for the predators to relish, they will probably stay around long enough to cover their initial cost—and some do take up permanent residence.

These biological controls go a long way in keeping your garden clean. The predators, of which the *praying mantis* is a prime example, feed upon other insects by using their sharp mouth parts: beaks, mandibles and jaws.

The popular *ladybug* is really a beetle and is a voracious eater of aphids, mealybugs and other destructive pests. The larvae have an even hardier appetite than their parents. Ladybugs are very efficient because they can get into even the tightest places in order to seek their prey. The average adult consumes about six hundred aphids a week; the larvae eat twice as many.

Aphid lions include *ant lions, dobson flies* and the wonderful *lacewings*. Lacewings belong to an order of insects with soft bodies and veined, gauzelike wings. They are generally nocturnal and provide excellent control of scale, thrips, aphids, mealybugs and caterpillars.

Ambush bugs, assassin bugs and *damsel bugs* are other beneficial creatures that do a world of good in the garden by attacking and killing dozens of various harmful insects.

Included in the biological control arsenal are *insect parasites*. Generally, the larvae of these insects enter the body of their host and feed on its tissues until they are nearly grown. When the host expires, the parasites may continue their existence in the dead host or may pupate elsewhere. Such parasites have a tremendous ability to find host organisms and can produce more females under adverse conditions than males, thus ensuring a greater number of offspring in the next generation.

Parasitic wasps are among the most valuable of the predators. Almost all species are beneficial. The *ichneumonid fly*, really a wasp, is smaller than the *braconid wasp* and can inhabit many species of hosts. These little devils lay their eggs in or near the body of the host so that the emerging larvae can find food. When they hatch, the larvae feed on the host internally.

Chalcid wasps are very tiny predatory insects that attack the eggs, larval and pupal forms of insect pests such as scale, mealybugs, aphids, flies and beetles. They will occur naturally in your garden (as will other good bugs) unless you have previously used commercial poison sprays. Another very important wasp the gardener should know about is the *trichogramma wasp*, a potent destroyer of many insect eggs that kills its host before the host can damage the plant. The trichogramma itself will not harm or feed on vegetation.

BENEFICIAL BIRDS

Do not forget birds when considering ways of ridding your garden of insect pests. Each day a chickadee eats from two hundred to five hundred insects; a brown thrasher eats over six hundred insects; and a house wren feeds five hundred caterpillars and spiders to its young.

Other helpful birds include bobolinks, meadowlarks, doves, field sparrows, purple martins, swallows and black phoebes. These birds are very helpful. Even if some birds damage berries and fruits, the good birds will always outnumber the bad ones.

Some birds prefer special insect fare; others are indiscriminate vacuum cleaners. Of the many birds that visit gardens, chickadees, house wrens, towhees and phoebes are among the best insect eaters. Swallows depend almost entirely on insects for food. They have large throats and sweep the sky clean of nocturnal insects. The purple martin, a swallow, is perhaps the most beneficial to man. Baltimore orioles will consume an array of insect pests that includes caterpillers, beetles and ants. Cuckoos also take care of a long list of destructive plant pests. The kingbird of the flycatcher family is a priceless ally in the garden, and woodpeckers take care of many wood-destroying insects. The towhee picks off hibernating beetles and larvae, and meadowlarks not only eat insects but also eliminate some weeds from the garden.

I always try to keep birds in my garden. To attract birds to your garden, plant shrubs they like, keep water in bird baths for them and install bird houses.

Plants that Attract Birds to the Small Garden

Here is a list of shrubs, vines and trees to attract birds to your garden:

SHRUBS

Bayberry (*Myrica* spp.)
Blueberry (*Vaccinium* spp.)
Buckthorn (*Rhamnus* spp.)
Coral berry (*Ardisia crenata*)
Dogwood (*Cornus* spp.)
Honeysuckle (*Lonicera* spp.)
Inkberry (*Ilex glabra*)
Winterberry (*Ilex verticillata*)

VINES

Bittersweet (*Celastrus* spp.)
Greenbrier (*Smilax* spp.)
Halls honeysuckle (*Lonicera japonica* 'Halliana')

Virginia creeper
(Parthenocissus
quinquefolia)
Wild grape (Vitis spp.)

TREES

Alder (Alnus spp.)
Ash (Fraxinus spp.)

Birch (Betula spp.)
Flowering crab
apple (Malus spp.)
Hawthorn
(Crataegus spp.)
Maple (Acer spp.)
Mulberry (Morus
spp.)

PEST-EATING BIRDS

Here are some of the best birds for insect protection:

Baltimore oriole

Barn swallow

Black-capped chickadee

Brown thrasher

Crested flycatcher

House wren

Meadowlark

Mockingbird

Phoebe

Purple martin

Song sparrow

Tufted titmouse

Wood thrush

SOPHISTICATED INSECT PREVENTATIVES

In the last decade many new ways of combatting insects in the garden have emerged to replace using any chemicals in your fight with plant pests. Perhaps one of the most unique approaches is the sterile male technique, which requires producing male insects that are sterile and releasing them in mass. Native males then stand a poor chance of reaching the females ahead of their sterile competitors. (This method requires release with each generation of insects.) After a number of releases of sterile males it is possible that only infertile eggs will be produced by females.

The United States Department of Agriculture researchers claim that sex attractants offer the greatest possibility for the development of effective specific ways of controlling some insects. These attractants include insect lures, chemicals or light that evokes a visual response from insects. The sex attractants are used to lure male insects into traps where they are killed. This process has worked well with the gypsy moth.

Appendix

FOR MORE PLANT INFORMATION

The following groups are also good sources of information on plant conservation and general horticultural subjects. Write them for membership information and fees.

Brooklyn Botanic Garden
1000 Washington Ave.
Brooklyn, NY 11225

The Farallones Institute
The Rural Center
15290 Coleman Valley Rd.
Occidental, CA 95465

Gardens for All
Dept. FG
180 Flynn Ave.
Burlington, VT 05401

Herb Society of America
300 Massachusetts Ave.
Boston, MA 02115

National Audubon
Society
950 Third Ave.
New York, NY 10022

National Wildlife
Federation
1412 16th St., N.W.
Washington, DC 20036

Sierra Club
530 Bush St.
San Francisco, CA 94108

PLANT SOCIETIES

You can write to these plant societies for information on membership, which usually includes a bulletin or magazine (monthly or semi-monthly). Some societies have library books available, distribute seed and hold conventions. Prices listed are membership fees as of January, 1993.

American Boxwood
Society ($15)
Blandy Experimental
Farm
P.O. Box 85
Boyce, VA 22620

American Camellia
Society ($17.50)
Dr. C. David Schiebert
P.O. Box 1217
Fort Valley, GA 31030-
1217

American Conifer Society
($20)
Maxine Schwarz
P.O. Box 242
Severna Park, MD 21146

American Dahlia Society
($8)
Michael Martinolich
159 Pine St.
New Hyde Park, NY 11040

American Fuchsia Society
($12.50)
San Francisco County Fair
Bldg.
Ninth Ave. & Lincoln Way
San Francisco, CA 94122

American Hemerocallis
Society ($18)
Elly Launius
1454 Rebel Dr.
Jackson, MS 39211

American Hibiscus Society
($13)
P.O. Drawer 321540
Cocoa Beach, FL 32932

American Hosta Society
($12.50)
Jack A. Freedman
3103 Heatherhill Dr.
Huntsville, AL 35802

American Iris Society
($9.50)
Carol Ramsey
6518 Beachy Ave.
Wichita, KS 67206

American Peony Society
($7.50)
Greta M. Kessenich
250 Interlachen Rd.
Hopkins, MN 55343

American Rhododendron
Society ($25)
Paula L. Cash
14885 S.W. Sunrise Ln.
Tigard, OR 97224

American Rose Society
($25)
P.O. Box 30000
Shreveport, LA 71130

Azalea Society of
America ($15)
Marjorie Taylor
P.O. Box 6244
Silver Spring, MD 20901

Cactus and Succulent
Society of America ($20)
Virginia F. Martin
2631 Fairgreen Ave.
Arcadia, CA 93130

The Delphinium Society
($6)
Shirley E. Bassett
Takakkaw
Ice House Wood
Oxted, Surrey, RH8
9DW, England

Gardenia Society of
America ($5)
Lyman Duncan
P.O. Box 879
Atwater, CA 95301

Herb Society of America
($35)
9019 Kirtland Chardon Rd.
Mentor, OH 44060

Hobby Greenhouse
Association ($10)
Janice L. Hale
8 Glen Terr.
Bedford, MA 01730

Hydroponic Society of America ($25)
Gene Brisbon
P.O. Box 6067
Concord, CA 94524

International Camellia Society ($9)
Edith Mazzei
1486 Yosemite Cir.
Concord, CA 94521

International Clematis Society
Hildegard Widmann-Evison
Buford House, Tenbury Wells
Worcester WR15 8HQ, England

International Geranium Society ($12.50)
Mrs. Robin Schultz
5861 Walnut Dr.
Eureka, CA 95501

International Lilac Society, Inc. ($10)
Walter W. Oakes
P.O. Box 315
Rumford, ME 04276

Magnolia Society ($15)
Phelan A. Bright
907 S. Chestnut St.
Hammond, LA 70403-5102

National Chrysanthemum Society ($12)
Galen L. Goss
5012 Kingston Dr.
Annandale, VA 22003

National Fuchsia Society ($14)
Mrs. Mildred Elliott
15103 McRae
Norwalk, CA 90650

North American Lily Society ($12.50)
Dorothy B. Schaefer
P.O. Box 476
Waukee, IA 50263

Perennial Plant Association ($35)
Steven Still
3383 Schirtzinger Rd.
Columbus, OH 43026

STATE AGRICULTURAL EXTENSION SERVICES

This service is the combined effort of the county government, the state college or university responsible for agriculture and the U.S. Department of Agriculture. Telephone numbers and addresses for these services will be found under the county government listings in your local telephone directories. The Agricultural Extension Service is the most up-to-date and extensive source of information on horticultural subjects in the United States. Circulars or bulletins answering frequently asked questions about gardening are generally available in printed form for the asking. Addresses of these offices follow:

Auburn University
Auburn, AL 36830

College of Agriculture
University of Arizona
Tucson, AZ 85721

University of Arkansas
P. O. Box 391
Little Rock, AR 72203

Agricultural Extension
Service
2200 University Ave.
Berkeley, CA 94720

Colorado State University
Fort Collins, CO 80521

College of Agriculture
University of Connecticut
Storrs, CT 06268

College of Agricultural
Sciences
University of Delaware
Newark, DE 19711

University of Florida
217 Rolfs Hall
Gainesville, FL 32601

College of Agriculture
University of Georgia
Athens, GA 30602

University of Hawaii
2500 Dole St.
Honolulu, HI 96822

College of Agriculture
University of Idaho
Moscow, ID 83843

College of Agriculture
University of Illinois
Urbana, IL 61801

Agricultural
Administration Building
Purdue University
Lafayette, IN 47907

Iowa State University
Ames, IA 50010

Kansas State University
Manhattan, KS 66502

College of Agriculture
University of Kentucky
Lexington, KY 40506

Louisiana State University
Knapp Hall, University
Station
Baton Rouge, LA 70803

Department of Public
Information
University of Maine
Orono, ME 04473

University of Maryland
Agricultural Division
College Park, MD 20742

Stockbridge Hall
University of
Massachusetts
Amherst, MA 01002

Department of Information
Service
109 Agricultural Hall
East Lansing, MI 48823

Institute of Agriculture
University of Minnesota
St. Paul, MN 55101

Mississippi State
University
State College, MS 39762

1-98 Agricultural Building
University of Missouri
Columbia, MO 65201

Office of Information
Montana State University
Bozeman, MT 59715

Dept. of Information
College of Agriculture
University of Nebraska
Lincoln, NE 68503

Agricultural
Communications Service
University of Nevada
Reno, NV 89507

Schofield Hall
University of
New Hampshire
Durham, NH 03824

College of Agriculture
Rutgers State University
New Brunswick, NJ 08903

New Mexico State
University
Drawer 3AI
Las Cruces, NM 88001

State College of Agriculture
Cornell University
Ithaca, NY 14850

North Carolina State
University
State College Station
Raleigh, NC 27607

North Dakota State
University
State University Station
Fargo, ND 58102

Ohio State University
2120 Fyffe Road
Columbus, OH 43210

Oklahoma State
Universityy
Stillwater, OK 74074

Oregon State Univer-
sity
206 Waldo Hall
Corvallis, OR 97331

Pennsylvania State
University
Armsby Building
University Park, PA
16802

University of Rhode
Island
16 Woodwall Hall
Kingston, RI 02881

Clemson University
Clemson, SC 29631

South Dakota State
University
University Station
Brookings, SD 57006

University of
Tennessee
P. O. Box 1071
Knoxville, TN 37901

Texas A & M
University
Services Building
College Station, TX
77843

Utah State University
Logan, UT 84321

University of Vermont
Burlington, VT 05401

Virginia Polytechnic
Institute
Blacksburg, VA 24061

Washington State
University
115 Wilson Hall
Pullman, WA 99163

West Virginia University
Evansdale Campus
Appalachian Center
Morgantown, WV 26506

University of Wisconsin
Madison, WI 53706

University of
Wyoming
P.O. Box 3354
Laramie, WY 82070

Federal Extension
Service
U.S. Department of
Agriculture
Washington, DC 20250

MAIL-ORDER SUPPLIERS

Write to these suppliers for information on prices, shipping, catalogs and available plants and products.

GENERAL PLANTS SUPPLIERS

Burgess Seed & Plant Co.
905 Four Seasons Rd.
Bloomington, IL 61701

Henry Field's Heritage
Gardens
1 Meadow Ridge Rd.
Shenandoah, IA 51601-
0700

Gurney Seed & Nursery Co.
Yankton, SD 57079

Herbst Brothers Seedsmen,
Inc.
1000 N. Main St.
Brewster, NY 10509

International Growers
Exchange, Inc.
16785 Harrison
Livonia, MI 48154

Inter-State Nurseries
Hamburg, IA 51644

J. W. Jung Seed & Nursery
Co.
335 S. High St.
Randolph, WI 53957

Kelly Nurseries
P.O. Box 800
Dansville, NY 14437-
0800

Krider Nursery
P. O. Box 29
Middlebury, IN 56540

Louisiana Nursery
Rt. 7, Box 43
Opelousas, LA 70570

May Nursery Company
P.O. Box 1312
2115 W. Lincoln Ave.
Yakima, WA 98907

Earl May Seed &
Nursery Co.
Shenandoah, IA 51603

J. E. Miller Nurseries
Canandaigua, NY 14424

Nichols Garden Nursery
1190 North Pacific
Highway
Albany, OR 97321

Spring Hill Nurseries
6523 N. Galena Rd.
P. O . Box 1758
Peoria, IL 61656

Stern Nurseries
Geneva, NY 14456

Tennessee Nursery &
Seed Co.
Tennessee Nursery Rd.
Cleveland, TN 37311

Wayside Gardens Co.
Hodges, SC 29695

White Flower Farm
Litchfield, CT 06759

SPECIALTY PLANT SUPPLIERS

BEGONIAS

Antonelli Bros.
2545 Capitola Rd.
Santa Cruz, CA 95062

Fairyland Begonia and
Lily Garden
1100 Griffith Rd.
McKinleyville, CA
95521

BULBS, CORMS, TUBERS

P. DeJager & Sons, Inc.
188 Asbury St.
S. Hamilton, MA 01982

John Scheppers, Inc.
63 Wall St.
New York, NY 10005

CHRYSANTHEMUMS

Dooley Gardens
Rt.l
Hutchinson, MN 55350

Huff's Gardens
P.O. Box 187
Burlington, KS 66839

Sunnyslope Gardens
8638 Huntington Dr.
San Gabriel, CA 91775

Thon's Garden Mums
4811 Oak St.
Crystal Lake, IL 60012

DAYLILIES

American Daylily &
Perennials
P. O . Box 210
Grain Valley, MO 64029

Lenington-Long Gardens
7007 Manchester Ave.
Kansas City, MO 64133

Saxton Gardens
1 First St.
Saratoga Springs, NY 12866

Seawright Gardens
134 Indian Hill
Carlisle, MA 01741

Wimberlyway Gardens
7024 N.W. 18th Ave.
Gainesville, FL 32605-
3237

IRISES

Comanche Acres Iris
Gardens
R.R. 1, Box 258
Gower, MO 64454

Cooley's Gardens, Inc.
P. O. Box 126
Silverton, OR 97381

Mid-America Iris Gardens
P.O. Box 12982
Oklahoma City, OK 73157

Schreiner's Gardens
3625 Quinaby Rd. N.E.
Salem, OR 97303

Gilbert H. Wild & Sons
Sarcoxie, MS 64862

LILIES

B & D Lilies
330 P St.
Port Townsend, WA 98368

Borbeleta Gardens
15974 Canby Ave., Rt. 5
Fairibault, MN 55021

Fairyland Begonia and Lily
Garden
1100 Griffith Rd.
McKinleyville, CA 95521

Oregon Bulb Farms
14071 N.E. Arndt Rd.
Aurora, OR 97002

Rex Bulb Farms
P.O. Box 774
Port Townsend, WA 98368

PERENNIALS

Bluebird Nursery
P. O. Box 460
Clarkson, NE 68629

Bluestone Perennials
7211 Middle Ridge Rd.
Madison, OH 44057

Busse Gardens
Rt. 2, Box 238
Cokato, MN 55321
(peonies, hostas, daylilies,
perennials)

Caprice Farm Nursery
15425 S.W. Pleasant Hill Rd.
Sherwood, OR 97140
(tree peonies, hostas,
daylilies)

Carroll Gardens
P.O. Box 310
Westminster, MD 21157

Crownsville Nursery
P.O. Box 797
Crownsville, MD 21032

Fairway Enterprises
114 The Fairway
Albert Lea, MN 56007

Holbrook Farm and
Nursery
Rt. 2, Box 223B
Fletcher, NC 28732

Klehm & Son Nursery
Rt. 5, Box 197 Penny Rd.
S. Barrington, IL 60010

Lamb Nurseries
E. 101 Sharp Ave.
Spokane, WA 99202

Milaegers
4838 Douglas Ave.
Racine, WI 53402

Putney Nursery, Inc.
Rt. 5
Putney, VT 05346

Rice Creek Gardens
1315 66th Ave. N.E.
Minneapolis, MN 55432

Rocknoll Nursery
9210 U.S. 50
Hillsboro, OH 45133-
8546

Savory's Gardens
5300 Whiting Ave.
Edina, MN 55435
(hostas)

Siskiyou Rare Plant
Nursery
2825 Cummings Rd.
Medford, OR 97501

Spring Hill Nurseries
6523 N. Galena Rd.
P.O. Box 1758
Peoria, IL 61656

Gilbert H. Wild & Son
Sarcoxie, MO 64862
(peonies, daylilies)

RHODODENDRONS, AZALEAS
The Bovees Nursery
1737 S.W. Coronado
Portland, OR 97219

Cardinal Nursery
Rt. 1, Box 316
State Rd., NC 28676

Carlson's Gardens
P. O. Box 305
South Salem, NY 10590

Greer Gardens
1280 Goodpasture
Island Rd.
Eugene, OR 97401

ROSES
Armstrong Nurseries
Ontario, CA 91764

Fred Edmunds Roses
6235 S.W. Kahle Rd.
Wilsonville, OR 97070

Jackson & Perkins Co.
Medford, OR 97501

The Mini Farm
Rt. 1, Box 501
Bon Aqua, TN 37025

Mini-Roses
P.O. Box 4255,
Station A
Dallas, TX 75208

Moore Miniature Roses
2519 Visalia Ave.
Visalia, CA 93277

Nor'East Miniature
Roses, Inc.
58 Hammond St.
Rowley, MA 01969
or
P.O. Box 473
Ontario, CA 91762

Pixie Treasures Miniature Rose Nursery
4121 Prospect Ave.
Yorba Linda, CA 92686

Roses of Yesterday and Today
802 Brown's Valley Rd.
Watsonville, CA 95076

Star Roses
West Grove, PA 19390

OTHER SPECIALTY PLANT SUPPLIERS

Fox Hill Farm
444 W. Michigan Ave.
P. O. Box 9
Parma, MI 49269
(herbs)

John Messelaar
Bulb Co., Inc.
P.O. Box 269
Ipswich, MA 01938

Mohn's, Inc.
P.O. Box 2301
Atascadero, CA 93423
(perennial hybrid poppies)

Musser Forests, Inc.
P.O. Box 340
Indiana, PA 15701
(evergreen & hardwood
seedling trees)

Plumeria People
P.O. Box 820014
Houston, TX 77282-0014

Prairie Nursery
P.O. Box 365
Westfield, WI 53964
(prairie flowers, grasses)

Sandy Mush Herb
Nursery
Rt. 2
Leicester, NC 28748

Shady Oaks Nursery
700 19th Ave. N.E.
Waseca, MN 56093
(northern & shade plants)

Swan Island Dahlias
P.O. Box 800
Canby, OR 97013

TyTy Plantation
Box 159
TyTy, GA 31795
(cannas, southern bulbs)

Mary Walker Bulb Co.
P.O. Box 256
Omega, GA 31775
(southern specialties)

GENERAL SEED SUPPLIERS

Banana Tree
715 Northampton St.
Easton, PA 18042
(tropical ornamentals)

John Brudy Exotics
3411 Westfield
Brandon, FL 33511-7736
(unusual tropicals)

W. Atlee Burpee & Co.
300 Park Ave.
Warminster, PA 18974

The Cook's Garden
P. O. Box 65
Londonderry, VT 05148
(salad & imported
vegetables)

The Country Garden
Rt. 2, Box 455A
Crivitz, WI 54114
(cut flowers)

Henry Field Seed &
Nursery Co.
407 Sycamore St.
Shenandoah, IA 51602

Gurney Seed & Nursery Co.
Yankton SD 57079

Harris Seeds Garden
Trends, Inc.
961 Lyell Ave.
Rochester, NY 14606

Hastings
P.O. Box 4274
Atlanta, GA 30302-4274

Jackson & Perkins Co.
P.O. Box 1028
Medford, OR 97501

Le Jardin du Gourmet
P. O. Box 32
West Danville, CT 05873
(herbs, shallots)

J. W. Jung Seed &
Nursery Co.
335 S. High St.
Randolph, WI 53957

Kitazawa Seed
Company
356 West Taylor St.
San Jose, CA 95110

Liberty Seed Co.
P.O. Box 806
New Philadelphia, OH
44663

Earl May Seed &
Nursery Co.
208 N. Elm St.
Shenandoah, IA 51603

Nichols Garden Nursery
1190 N. Pacific High-
way
Albany, OR 97321

George W. Park Seed
Co.
P.O. Box 31
Greenwood, SC 29647

Pinetree Garden Seeds
R.R. 1, Box 397
New Gloucester, ME 04260
(small quantity vegetables)

Clyde Robin Seed Co., Inc.
P.O. Box 2855
Castro Valley, CA 94546

Select Seeds
81 Stickney Hill Rd.
Union, CT 06076
(heritage perennials and
annual flowers)

Shepherd's Garden Seeds
7839 W. Zayante Rd.
Felton, CA 95018
(European vegetables)

R. H. Shumway's
P.O. Box 1
Graniteville, SC 29829
or
P.O. Box 777
Rockford, IL 61105
(use nearest address)

Stokes Seeds
Stokes Bldg.
Buffalo, NY 14240

Thompson & Morgan,
Inc.
Jackson, NJ 08527

Otis S. Twilley Seed
Co.
P.O. Box 65
Trevose, PA 19047

Wildflower Seed Co.
P.O. Box 406
St. Helena, CA 94574
(specialty wildflower
seed mixtures)

SUPPLIERS OF BENEFICIAL INSECTS

The following insectaries provide natural enemies of insect pests:

American Biological
Supply Co.
1330 Dillon Heights Ave.
P.O. Box 3149
Baltimore, MD 21228

Beneficial Insectary
14751 Oak Run Rd.
Oak Run, CA 96069

BioLogic
Box 177
Springtown Rd.
Willow Hill, PA 17271

Carolina Biological Supply
Co.
Burlington, NC
27215

Nature's Control
P. O. Box 35
Medford, OR 97501

Rincon Vitova
P. O. Box 45
Oak View, CA 93022

GARDEN TOOL AND EQUIPMENT SUPPLIERS

Country Home
Products
P. O. Box 89
Cedar Beach Rd.
Charlotte VT 05445

Cumberland
General Store
Rt. 3
Crossville, TN 38555

Denman & Co.
2913 Saturn St.
Brea, CA 92621

John Houchins &
Sons, Inc.
801 N. Main
Schulenburg, TX 78956

LaMotte Chemical Co.
P.O. Box 329
Chestertown, MD
21620

A. M. Leonard
6665 Spiker Rd.
Piqua, OH 45356

Mantis Mfg.
1458 County Line Rd.
Huntingdon
Valley, PA 19006

Walter Nicke
19 Columbus Tpk.
Hudson, NY 12534

Smith & Hawken
Tool Co.
68 Homer
Palo Alto, CA 94301

Troy Bilt Mfg.
102nd St. & 9th Ave.
Troy, NY 12180

Yardman
5389 W. 130th
Cleveland, OH 44111

Bibliography

The books in the following list are the ones that I have referred to over and over through the years. Some are old classics, some are revised editions, and some are relatively new. Most are available at libraries and at bookstores with good gardening sections. If you have trouble locating any, you may try checking with a local plant society; they often make books available or can refer you to places to find them. Because of space I cannot list all the books I would like to, especially the recent plethora of big color garden books, so if your favorite book is missing it is not deliberate. What you will find here are the books that I have found to be most helpful in my many years of gardening.

BULBS

Glattstein, Judy. *The Gardener's World of Bulbs*. Brooklyn, N.Y.: Brooklyn Botanic Garden, 1991.

Horton, Al. *All About Bulbs*. San Ramon, Calif.: Ortho Books, 1986.

James, Theodore. *Flowering Bulbs Indoors & Out*. New York: Macmillan Publishing Co., 1991.

Whiteside, Katherine. *Classic Bulbs: Hidden Treasures for the Modern Garden*. New York: Random House, 1992.

CITY GARDENING

Colby, Deirdre. *City Gardening*. New York: Simon & Schuster, 1988.

Riker, Tom. *City & Suburban Gardens: Frontyards, Backyards, Terraces, Rooftops & Window Boxes*. Englewood Cliffs, N.J.: Prentice-Hall, 1977.

Young, Linda, *The City Gardener's Handbook*. New York: Random House, 1990.

CONTAINER GARDENING

Hillier, Malcolm. *Book of Container Gardening*. New York: Simon & Schuster, 1991.

Joyce, David. *Hanging Baskets, Window Boxes, & Other Container Gardens: A Guide to Creative Small-Scale Gardening*. New York: Summit Books, 1991.

Taloumis, George. *Container Gardening*. New York: Brooklyn Botanic Garden, 1989.

DISEASES AND PESTS

Carr, Anna. *Rodale's Color Handbook of Garden Insects*. Emmaus, Pa.: Rodale Press, 1983.

Chaube, H. S. *Plant Disease Management: Principles & Practice*. Boca Raton, Fla.: CRC Press, Inc., 1991.

Cranshaw, Whitney. *Pests of the West*. Golden, Colo.: Fulcrum Publishing, 1992.

Debach, Paul. *Biological Control of Natural Enemies, Second Edition*. Cambridge, England: Cambridge University Press, 1991.

Hart, Rhonda M. *Bugs, Slugs & Other Thugs: Controlling Garden Pests Organically*. Powmall, Vt.: Storey Communications, Inc., 1991.

GREENHOUSE GARDENING

Edwards, Jonathan. *Greenhouse Gardening: Step by Step to Growing Success*. North Pomfret, Vt.: Trafalgar Square, 1991.

Hessayon, D. G. *Be Your Own Greenhouse Expert*. New York: Sterling Publishing Co., Inc., 1991.

Smith, Shane. *Greenhouse Gardener's Companion*. Golden, Colo.: Fulcrum Publishing, 1992.

LANDSCAPING AND PLANNING BOOKS

Brookes, John. *The Book of Garden Design*. New York: Macmillan Publishing Co., 1991.

Carter, Louise, and Joanne Lawson. *The Three Year Garden Journal*. Golden, Colo.: Starwood Publishing, 1992.

Eckbo, Garrett. *Urban Landscape Design*. New York: McGraw-Hill, 1964.

Hyams, Edward. *English Cottage Gardens*. New York: Viking Penguin, 1988.

Ireys, Alice Recknagel. *Designs for American Gardens: A Guide with Complete Plans, Growing Information, and Hundreds of Recommended Plants*. Englewood Cliffs, N.J.: Prentice Hall, 1991.

Ireys, Alice Recknagel. *Garden Design*. Englewood Cliffs, N.J.: Prentice Hall, 1991.

Johnson, Hugh. *The Principles of Gardening*. New York: Simon & Schuster, 1984.

Kramer, Jack. *Easy Gardening*. Golden, Colo.: Fulcrum Publishing, 1991.

Malitz, Jerome. *Personal Landscapes*. Portland, Oreg.: Timber Press, 1989.

Nelson, William R. *Planning Design: A Manual of Theory and Practice*. Champaign, Ill.: Stipes Publishing Co., 1985.

Reader's Digest Practical Guide to Home Landscaping. Pleasantville, N.Y.: Reader's Digest Association, 1972.

Saito, Katsuo. *Japanese Gardens*. New York: Charles E. Tuttle Co., 1971.

Smith, Ken. *Home Landscaping in the Northeast & Midwest*. New York: Price Stern Sloan, Inc., 1985.

Smith, Ken. *Southern Home Landscaping*. New York: Price Stern Sloan, Inc., 1982.

LILIES

Brown, M. Jefferson. *A Plantsman's Guide to Lilies.* New York: Sterling Publishing Co., 1991.

Jefferson-Brown, Michael. *The Lily: For Garden, Patio & Display.* North Pomfret, Vt.: Trafalgar Square, 1988.

ORGANIC GARDENING

Blake, Francis. *Organic Farming & Growing.* North Pomfret, Vt.: Trafalgar Square, 1991.

Hamilton, Geoff. *Organic Gardening.* New York: Random House, 1992.

Kitto, Dick. *Planning the Organic Vegetable Garden.* Golden, Colo.: Fulcrum Publishing, 1993.

Pike, Dave. *Organic Gardening: Step by Step to Growing Success.* North Pomfret, Vt.: Trafalgar Square, 1991.

Sunset Editors. *An Illustrated Guide to Organic Gardening.* Menlo Park, Calif.: Sunset Publishing Corp., 1991.

PATIO GARDENING

Kramer, Jack. *Patio Gardening.* New York: Price Stern Sloan, Inc., 1980.

Williams, Robin. *The Complete Book of Patio & Container Gardening.* New York: Sterling Publishing Co., Inc., 1991.

Yang, Linda. *The Terrace Gardener's Handbook: Raising Plants on a Balcony, Terrace, Rooftop, Penthouse or Patio.* Portland, Oreg.: Timber Press, 1982.

PERENNIALS AND ANNUALS

Clausen, Ruth Rogers, and Nicholas H. Ekstrom. *Perennials for American Gardens.* New York: Random House, 1989.

Garden Way Staff. *Using Annuals & Perennials.* Longmeadow Press, 1990.

McGourty, Frederick. *The Perennial Gardener.* Boston, Mass.: Houghton Mifflin, 1991.

McGourty, Frederick. *Perennials & Their Uses.* Brooklyn, N.Y.: Brooklyn Botanic Garden, 1989.

Sunset Magazine & Book Editors. *Garden Color: Annuals & Perennials.* Menlo Park, Calif.: Sunset Publishing Corp., 1981.

Wilson, Helen Van Pelt. *New Perennials Preferred.* New York: Macmillan Publishing Co., 1992.

PLANT PROPAGATION

Clarke, Graham, and Alan Toogood. *The Complete Book of Plant Propagation.* New York: Sterling Publishing Co., Inc., 1990.

Hartmann, Hudson T. and Dale E. Kester. *Plant Progagation—Principles and Practices, Fifth Edition.* Englewood Cliffs, N.J.: Prentice-Hall, 1990.

Hill, Lewis. *Secrets of Plant Propagation.* Powmall, Vt.: Storey Communications, Inc., 1985.

Thompson, Peter. *Creative Propagation: A Grower's Guide.* Portland, Oreg.: Timber Press, 1989.

PRUNING

Cook, Alan D. *Pruning Techniques.* Brooklyn, N.Y.: Brooklyn Botanic Gardens, 1991.

Joyce, David. *The Complete Guide to Pruning & Training Plants.* New York: Simon & Schuster, 1992.

REGIONAL BOOKS

Foley, Daniel J. *Gardening by the Sea.* Orleans, Mass.: Parnassus Imprints, 1982.

Hunt, William L. *Southern Garden, Southern Gardening.* Durham, N.C.: Duke University Press, 1982.

Schuler, Stanley. *How to Grow Almost Everything.* New York: Evans & Co., 1965.

Vick, Roger. *Gardening: Plains and Upper Midwest.* Golden, Colo.: Fulcrum Publishing, 1991.

ROSES

Ray, Richard, and Michael MacCaskey. *Roses.* New York: Price Stern Sloan, Inc., 1984.

Toogood, Alan. *Roses in Gardens.* New York: Sterling Publishing Co., Inc., 1990.

TREES AND SHRUBS

Bird, Richard. *Flowering Trees & Shrubs.* Hauppauge, N.Y.: Barron's Educational Series, Inc., 1989.

Brazell, Margaret. *Growing Trees on the Great Plains.* Golden, Colo.: Fulcrum Publishing, 1992.

Frederick, William H., Jr. *100 Great Garden Plants.* Portland, Oreg.: Timber Press, 1986.

Gardiner, James M. *Magnolias.* Chester, Conn.: Globe Pequot, 1989.

Harris, Richard W. *Arboriculture: Care of Trees, Shrubs & Vines in the Landscape,* 2nd ed. Englewood Cliffs, N.J.: Prentice Hall, 1991.

Hessayon, D. G. *The Tree & Shrub Expert.* New York: Sterling Publishing Company, Inc., 1990.

The Hillier Manual of Trees & Shrubs. North Pomfret, Vt.: Trafalgar Square, 1991.

Taffler, Stephen. *Climbing Plants & Wall Shrubs.* North Pomfret, Vt.: Trafalgar Square, 1991.

Wyman, Donald. *Trees for American Gardens.* New York: Macmillan Publishing Co., 1969.

Zucker, Isabel. *Flowering Shrubs and Small Trees.* New York: Grove/Weidenfeld, 1990.

VINES, GROUND COVERS, AND LAWNS

Foley, Daniel J. *Ground Covers for Easier Gardening.* Mineola, N.Y.: Dover Publications, 1972.

Fretwell, Barry O. *Clematis.* Deer Park, Wis.: Capability's Books, 1989.

Wyman, Donald. *Shrubs and Vines for American Gardens.* New York: Macmillan Publishing Co., 1970.

Index

127